COOKING

WITH THE

HORSE & BUGGY PEOPLE

A COLLECTION OF
OVER 600 FAVORITE AMISH RECIPES FROM
THE HEART OF HOLMES COUNTY

Carlisle Press
WALNUT CREEK

First Printing		1986
Second Printing		1987
Third Printing		1988
Fourth Printing		1990
Fifth Printing		1991
Sixth Printing (first revised)		1994
Seventh Printing	November	1994
Eighth Printing	June	1995
Ninth Printing	December	1995
Tenth Printing	August	1996
Eleventh Printing	March	1997
Twelfth Printing	October	1997
Thirteenth Printing	December	1997
Fourteenth Printing	September	1998
Fifteenth Printing	August	1999
Sixteenth Printing	February	2000
Seventeenth Printing	August	2000
Eighteenth Printing	January	2001
Nineteenth Printing	October	2001
Twentieth Printing	July	2002
Twenty-first Printing	March	2003
Twenty-second Printing	December	2003
Twenty-third Printing	May	2005
Twenty-fourth Printing	September	2005
Twenty-fifth Printing	September	2006

ISBN 1-890050-16-4
Printed by Carlisle Printing of Walnut Creek
Artwork – Troyer Arts, Millersburg, Ohio

2673 Twp. Rd. 421
Sugarcreek, Ohio 44681
330-852-1900

Carlisle Press
WALNUT CREEK

Preface

Welcome to *Cooking with the Horse & Buggy People,* a collection of over 600 favorite Amish recipes. The Amish ladies from Holmes County, Ohio, are delighted to pass on this rich culinary heritage to you.

You'll love the wholesomeness you experience when you prepare these main dishes and soups or browse through the canning section.

The delightful taste of the mouthwatering desserts the Amish are so well known for will delight even the most discriminating palate.

We are confident that *Cooking with the Horse & Buggy People* will help you achieve excellence in Amish style food preparation!

A sincere thank-you to the families who shared their favorite recipes in the following pages.

Marvin Wengerd

Contents

Thumb Index

Each of the 14 different
categories in this cookbook are designated
with a "thumb finder."

Simply fan the front edge
of the book and find the page
that corresponds with
the solid bar on this page.

Abbreviations Used

T.	tablespoon
t.	teaspoon
C.	cup
qt.	quart
pt.	pint
lb.	pound
oz.	ounce

Breads

Cakes

Cookies

Desserts

Pies

Salads

Main Dishes

Soups

Cereal, Etc.

Candy

Miscellaneous

Drinks

Canning, Etc.

Home Remedies &
Preparing Wild Game

- Notes -

Breads

Wheat Oatmeal Bread

3 T. yeast, soaked in 1 C. warm water
2/3 C. cane molasses
2/3 C. shortening or cooking oil
2 C. rolled oats
2 C. wheat flour

8 C. flour
4 t. salt
1 T. lecithin
3 C. warm water

Soak yeast in warm water. Add 3 C. warm water, salt, lecithin and molasses. Add flour and oats. Knead then add cooking oil. Let rise until double. Work down and shape loaves. Let rise in pans and bake at 300° for 25-30 minutes. Makes 3 or 4 loaves.

Mrs. John A. Weaver

2 Hour Buns

1 1/2 pkg. yeast
1 C. warm water

1/4 C. white sugar
1 egg

Beat these ingredients until foamy then add 2 T. shortening, 1/2 t. salt and about 3 1/2 C. bread flour. Mix and knead just enough to blend well. Let rise till double in size, shape into buns, let rise again and bake at 400° for 15-20 minutes. These can be made in 2 hours.

Mrs. Adam Yoder
Mrs. Dan C. Yoder

Golden Cake Bread

1 C. milk, scalded
1/2 C. sugar
    Cook these 3 ingredients then cool.

1/2 C. margarine

1 T. dry yeast
    Dissolve yeast in warm water.

1/4 C. warm water

2 beaten eggs
2 t. vanilla

1 t. salt
4 to 4 1/2 C. flour

Beat well, let rise 1 hour. Punch down, let rise 3/4 hour. Makes 2 loaves. Bake 35 minutes at 350°.

Mrs. Viola Miller

Soft Oatmeal Rolls

1 C. quick oatmeal
2 C. boiling water
   Cook this together and let cool. Pour over:

3 T. oleo

$^2/_3$ C. brown sugar
1 $^1/_2$ t. salt

2 T. dry yeast
$^1/_3$ C. warm water
1 T. white sugar

Dissolve yeast in warm water and mix all together. Add 5 C. of bread flour, one cup at a time. Let rise once, then work out and spread with melted oleo, brown sugar and cinnamon. Roll out and cut. Bake at 350°. Frost with your favorite frosting.

Mary Ann Yoder

Cinnamon Rolls

Soften: 1 pkg. yeast
          1 C. scalded milk, cool to lukewarm, add yeast
Add: $^1/_4$ C. white sugar
          1 C. flour
When cool add: 1 t. salt
                    2 beaten eggs
                    $^1/_4$ C. melted butter
                    1 $^1/_2$ C. flour

Mix well and let rise. Roll out and spread with $^1/_4$ C. brown sugar and 1 t. cinnamon. Bake at 425° for 8 to 10 minutes.

Mrs. Roman E. Raber

Pumpkin Bread

$^2/_3$ C. lard
$2^2/_3$ C. sugar
2 C. pumpkin
$^2/_3$ C. water
$3^1/_3$ C. flour
2 t. soda
$^2/_3$ C. raisins

1 $^1/_2$ t. salt
1 $^1/_2$ t. baking powder
1 t. cinnamon
1 t. cloves
$^2/_3$ C. nuts
4 eggs

Cream lard and sugar until fluffy. Add remaining ingredients and pour into pans. Bake at 350° for 70 minutes or until done. Makes 2 loaves.

Mrs. Henry E. Mast

Honey Bread

2 C. quick oatmeal
2½ C. boiling water
4 eggs, beaten
2 T. salt
1 C. honey

1 T. Crisco
3 pkg. yeast
3 C. warm water
14 C. flour

Add boiling water to oatmeal, set aside until lukewarm. Mix yeast and water. Add honey, eggs, salt and Crisco to oatmeal mixture then add yeast, water and flour. Knead well, let rise, knead again and form into loaves. Bake at 325° for 50 min.

Mrs. Mary Yoder

Granny Bread

Dissolve:
2 pkg. yeast
1 t. sugar
½ C. lukewarm water

Add:
2 C. warm water
½ C. sugar or ⅓ C. honey
1 T. salt
½ C. lard

¾ C. whole wheat flour
¾ C. oatmeal
6-7 C. Robin Hood flour
    (unbleached)

Mix and let rise. Knead and let rise again, then divide into greased bread pans. Let rise. Bake at 350° for 30 minutes or until golden brown. Makes 3 loaves.

Mom's White Bread

Dissolve:
3 T. yeast
1 C. warm water
1 C. white sugar

2 pt. water (scant)
1½ T. lecithin (optional)
13 C. flour

Add:
¾ C. oleo or cooking oil
1 t. salt

Mix and let rise. Knead and let rise, then divide in loaves. Let rise. Bake at 350° for 30 minutes.

Mrs. John A. Weaver

10

Very Good Brown Bread

⅓ C. brown sugar	2 T. yeast
⅓ C. white sugar	pinch of salt
3 T. flour	¾ C. oil
1 C. boiling water	2 C. whole wheat flour
2 C. cold water	6 C. Robin Hood flour

Mix first five ingredients together. Boil until sugar is dissolved. Cool to lukewarm. Add yeast and salt. Let set till yeast starts to work. Add oil and flour, knead well. Let rise, knead down every 15 minutes for 1 hour. Makes 4 loaves. Bake at 325° for 35 minutes.

Mrs. Eli A. Beachy

Bread

¾ C. sugar (½ white, ½ brown)
¾ C. flour
1 T. salt

Mix and add 3 C. warm water. Stir well and add 2 T. dry yeast. Let set till it starts to rise, add 2 T. honey and ¾ C. oil. Mix well. Then add 7 to 8 cups flour. 1 to 3 cups whole wheat flour may be used. Knead well. Cover and let rise. Punch down. Let rise again. Divide in loaves and let rise. Bake at 350° for 30 minutes or until nicely browned. Makes 4 loaves.

Mary Schlabach

Cinnamon Bread

2 C. scalded milk (cool to lukewarm)
2 pkg. yeast, soaked in ½ C. warm water

¾ to 1 C. white sugar	2 t. salt
½ C. shortening	2 beaten eggs
8-10 C. flour	

Mix cooled milk with sugar and shortening. Add yeast mixture, salt, beaten eggs and flour. Knead well. Let rise, work down and let rise again. Roll out and spread with melted butter. Sprinkle with brown sugar and cinnamon. Roll up and put in loaf pans. Let rise, bake at 350° for 30-35 minutes. Delicious.

Mrs. John A. Miller

Oatmeal Whole Wheat Bread

4 C. rolled oats (quick)
1 C. brown sugar or honey
2 C. whole wheat flour

1 stick oleo
4 T. salt
3 pkg. yeast

Mix all the above ingredients except for yeast. Add 8 C. boiling water. Mix and cool to lukewarm. Dissolve yeast in 2 C. warm water and add to batter. Add 18-20 C. bread flour. Let rise until double, punch down. Let rise again till double, punch down and put in pans. Bake at 350° until nice and brown. Makes 6-7 loaves.

Mrs. Andy C. Yoder

Oatmeal Bread

1 C. quick oats
1/2 C. whole wheat flour
1/2 C. salad oil

1/4 C. brown sugar
1 T. salt
2 C. hot water

Mix and cool to lukewarm. Dissolve 1 T. (1 pkg.) dry yeast in 1/2 C. lukewarm water and add to batter. Add 1 C. all-purpose flour, mix well and let set until bubbly. Add approximately 4 C. all-purpose flour or enough flour until thick enough to knead and make a smooth and elastic dough. Place in greased bowl and let rise until double in bulk. Punch down and let rise again. Shape into 2 loaves, place in greased loaf pans. Let rise till double. Bake at 350° for 30 minutes.

Mrs. Viola Miller

Rolls

1 C. milk
1 C. hot water
1/4 C. white sugar
2 T. butter
pinch of salt

Dissolve 2 1/2 T. yeast in
1/2 C. warm water
3 C. doughnut mix
3 C. flour

Scald milk. Add hot water. Pour over sugar, butter and salt. Cool to lukewarm. Add yeast mixture, doughnut mix and flour. Mix and let rise until double in bulk. Roll out and spread with soft butter, brown sugar and cinnamon. Roll as jelly roll. Slice 1" thick, put on cookie sheet. Let rise again. Bake at 350°.

Mrs. Dan Erb

Donuts and Rolls

1 C. scalded milk
¼ C. sugar
4½ C. flour
⅓ C. Crisco

2 eggs
1 t. salt
1 pkg. yeast
¼ C. warm water

Mix yeast with warm water. Mix milk, sugar, salt and 1 C. flour and beat until smooth. Add Crisco and beat. Add eggs, yeast and remaining flour. Knead 10-15 minutes and let rise 1 hour. Punch down. Form into rolls or donuts.

Glaze

1½ lb. powdered sugar
¼ C. hot water
1 T. Crisco

1 t. vanilla
1 pkg. Knox gelatine

Dissolve Knox gelatine in ¼ C. cold water. If glaze is too thick, add more hot water.

Mrs. Henry E. Mast

Gingerbread

1 C. flour
1 C. whole wheat flour
1 T. ginger
1 t. soda
½ t. salt

½ C. molasses
½ C. butter
½ C. water
1 egg

Preheat oven to 325°. Mix flours, ginger, soda and salt. Combine molasses, butter and water in saucepan and bring to a boil. Mix with dry ingredients and add egg. Pour into well greased pan and bake 25-30 minutes. Serve with whipped cream and butterscotch syrup.

Mrs. Henry E. Mast

Rolls

1 C. milk, scalded
1 stick oleo
⅓ C. sugar
½ t. salt

2 eggs
1 pkg. yeast, dissolved in
  ¼ C. warm water
4 C. flour (scant)

Scald milk and pour over oleo, sugar and salt. Cool to lukewarm then add eggs, yeast mixture and flour. Refrigerate dough overnight. Let rise until double in bulk. Roll out and spread with butter, brown sugar and cinnamon. Roll like jelly roll. Cut into 1" slices, put on cookie sheet. Let rise until almost double in size. Bake at 350° until lightly browned. Take out, cool and frost.

13

Mrs. Henry J.C. Yoder

Pull Buns

1 pkg. yeast, dissolved in
   1/4 C. lukewarm water
1 C. scalded milk
1/3 C. butter, melted

1/2 t. salt
3 eggs, well beaten
1/3 C. sugar
3 3/4 C. flour

Sugar Mixture

3/4 C. sugar
1/2 C. ground nutmeats

3 t. cinnamon

Mix sugar, butter, salt and scalded milk and let cool to lukewarm. Add yeast, eggs and flour to make a stiff batter. Cover and let rise until double in bulk. Knead and let rise again. Make dough into small balls about the size of walnuts and dip in melted butter and roll in sugar mixture. Pile balls loosely in ungreased angel food pan and let rise again for 30 minutes. Bake at 400° for 10 minutes then at 350° for approximately 30 minutes or until brown. Turn pan upside down on plate.

Mrs. Mose Nisley

Buns

1 C. hot water
1/2 C. sugar

1 T. salt
3 T. butter

Mix and cool to lukewarm and add:

2 T. yeast, dissolved in
   3/4 C. warm water
1 egg, well beaten

5 3/4 C. flour

Knead and grease dough and cover with waxed paper. Let rise 2 hours or until double in bulk. Work out in small balls and let rise. Bake at 375° for 25-30 minutes. Do not overbake. You can keep dough one week in refrigerator for later use.

Mrs. Jonas N. Borntrager

14

Elephant Ears

1½ C. milk
6 T. shortening
2 pkg. yeast
2 T. sugar

1 t. salt
4 C. flour
oil for frying

Sugar Mixture

½ C. sugar

1 t. cinnamon

In a saucepan combine milk, sugar, salt and shortening and heat until shortening is melted. Do not let mixture boil. Cool mixture to lukewarm. Add yeast and stir until dissolved. Stir in flour (2 C. at a time). Beat after each addition until smooth. Put in a greased bowl, cover with damp cloth and let rise until double. Pinch off pieces of dough about the size of a golf ball. Stretch each piece into a thin 6-8 inch circle. Fry one at a time in oil heated to 350° until dough rises to the surface. Turn and fry on other side until light brown. Drain on paper towel and sprinkle with sugar mixture.

Miss Verna L. Miller

Zucchini Bread

3 eggs
1 C. cooking oil
2 C. white sugar
2 C. peeled shredded zucchini
3 t. vanilla
3 C. flour

1 t. salt
1 t. soda
3 t. cinnamon
¼ t. baking powder
½ t. chopped nuts

Beat eggs till foamy. Add oil, sugar, zucchini and vanilla. Mix lightly but well. Add flour, salt, soda, cinnamon, baking powder and nuts. Mix together and divide batter in 2 greased loaf pans. Bake at 325° for 1 hour.

Mrs. David E. Hershberger
Mary Ellen Troyer
Mrs. Marlin Yoder
Mrs. William Byler
Mrs. J.L. Miller

15

- *Notes* -

Cakes

Hickory Nut Cake

3 eggs, separated
1½ C. sugar
2¼ C. sifted cake flour
3 t. baking powder
1 t. salt

⅓ C. Wesson oil
1 C. water
vanilla or maple flavoring
¾ C. chopped hickory nuts

Beat egg whites until foamy. Gradually add ½ C. sugar. Beat until stiff and glossy. In separate bowl sift remaining sugar, flour, baking powder and salt. Add oil, water, egg yolks and flavoring. Beat until smooth. Fold in meringue. Add nuts last. Bake in loaf or layer pans at 350°.

Mrs. Alvin H. Hershberger

Lazy Wife Cake

1½ C. pastry flour
3 T. cocoa
1 t. soda

pinch of salt
1 C. white sugar

Combine the above ingredients in sifter and sift into bowl. Mix with fork (no spoon) and make 3 holes in dry ingredients. In one hole put 1 t. vanilla, in another hole 7 T. cooking oil and in third hole 1 T. vinegar. Pour 1 C. cold water over mixture and mix thoroughly with fork. Bake at 350° for 25-30 minutes.

Katie N. Miller

Spice Cake

2 C. brown sugar
½ C. oleo
1 C. sour milk
2 eggs
1 t. cinnamon

1 t. cloves
1 t. allspice
1 t. soda
2 C. flour

Cream oleo and brown sugar. Add milk and eggs. Beat, then add remaining ingredients. Bake at 350° for 25-30 minutes.

Mrs. Marlin Yoder

Texas Sheet Cake

2 sticks oleo	½ t. salt
1 C. water	1 t. soda
4 T. cocoa	2 eggs, beaten
2 C. sugar	½ C. sour cream
2 C. flour	1 t. vanilla

Melt oleo in saucepan, add water and cocoa. Bring to boil. Add remaining ingredients, stirring lightly. Pour into greased cookie sheet. Bake at 350° for 15-20 minutes.

Icing

1 stick oleo	2 C. powdered sugar
4 T. cocoa	½ C. nuts
6 T. milk	1 t. vanilla

Melt oleo, add cocoa and milk and bring to boil. Add remaining ingredients and spread on cake.

Mrs. Mart R. Miller

Pineapple Sheet Cake

2 eggs	2 t. soda
2 C. white sugar	½ C. pecans
1 t. vanilla	½ (no. 2) can crushed
2 C. flour	pineapple

Beat eggs. Add sugar, vanilla and soda. Beat well. Add flour, pecans and pineapple. Bake at 350° for 25-30 minutes.

Icing

6 oz. cream cheese	½ C. chopped nuts
1 lb. powdered sugar	½ stick oleo (4 T.)
1 t. vanilla	

Have cream cheese at room temperature. Beat in powdered sugar, vanilla and oleo at room temperature. Add nuts last. Spread on cooled cake.

Mrs. Albert M. Yoder

Texas Sheet Cake

1. 2 C. white sugar
   2 C. flour
   ½ t. salt
2. 1 stick oleo
   1 C. hot water
   4 t. cocoa

3. 2 eggs, beaten
   ½ C. sour milk
   1 T. vinegar
   1 t. vanilla
   1 t. soda

Mix 1 to 3, then add 2. Bake in cookie sheet at 375° for 20 minutes.

Mrs. Aden J. Raber
Mrs. Henry M. Troyer

Candied Fruitcake

2 C. flour
1 C. white sugar
2 t. baking powder
³/₄ lb. dates
1 lb. candied fruit

½ t. salt
¼ t. cinnamon
4 eggs
1 lb. pecan halves

Sift flour, baking powder, salt and spice in bowl; add fruit and dates. Mix well with hands to coat each piece with flour. Beat eggs till foamy and add sugar in gradually. Add to fruit and mix well. Mix in nuts and put into greased pans lined with wax paper. Press mixture down firmly and decorate top with whole nuts and cherries. Bake at 250°-275° for approximately 1½ hours. Let stand for five minutes. Remove and brush top with white Karo. When cold wrap well and keep in cool place.

Mattie Hershberger

Mississippi Mud Cake

2 C. sugar
1 C. shortening
4 eggs
1½ C. flour
⅓ C. cocoa

¼ t. salt
1 t. vanilla
1 C. coconut
1 C. nuts

Bake in cookie sheet pan at 300° for 40-45 minutes. Spread marshmallows on top as soon as removed from oven. Spread icing on while hot.

Icing

1 lb. powdered sugar
⅓ C. cocoa
¼ lb. oleo, melted

½ C. milk
1 C. nuts

Melt oleo, add cocoa, milk and powdered sugar. Spread on cake while still hot. Sprinkle with nuts.

Mrs. Henry E. Mast

Chocolate Town Special Cake

1¾ C. sugar
⅔ C. lard
2 eggs
1 t. vanilla
2½ C. flour

1½ t. soda
½ t. salt
1 C. buttermilk
½ C. Hershey's cocoa
½ C. boiling water

Preheat oven to 350°. Grease and flour pan. Cream sugar and lard together until light and fluffy. Add eggs, one at a time, beating well after each addition, add vanilla. Sift together flour, baking soda and salt and add alternately with the buttermilk. Make heavy, smooth paste of the cocoa and boiling water, cool slightly, add and blend well. Pour into prepared pans and bake for about 35 minutes or until done.

Mrs. Henry E. Mast

Coffee Cake

1 C. oleo	2 t. soda
2 C. white sugar	1 t. salt
2 eggs	2 C. sour milk
2 t. baking powder	4 C. flour

Topping

1/3 C. brown sugar	1 t. cinnamon
1/3 C. flour	1/2 C. chopped nuts
3 T. butter, melted	

Mix dough and put half in 4 pie pans or cake pan. Mix topping and divide in half and put over dough. Put remaining dough on top with remaining topping. Bake at 350° for 25 minutes. Makes 4 coffee cakes. See below for filling recipe.

Mrs. Dannie H. Burkholder

Coffee Cake

1 C. milk	1 t. salt
1 stick oleo	2 eggs, beaten
1/2 C. sugar	1 pkg. yeast, dissolved in
3 1/2-4 C. flour	1/2 C. warm water

Heat milk to lukewarm. Cream sugar and oleo. Add eggs, salt, yeast mixture, milk and flour. Let rise once and put in three 9" cake pans. Put topping on top and let set 30 minutes. Bake at 375°. Cool. Split each cake in center to make 2 layers and put filling in between.

Topping

1/3 C. brown sugar	1 t. cinnamon
1/3 C. flour	1/2 C. chopped nuts
3 T. butter, melted	

Filling

Cook 3 round t. flour in 1 C. milk until thick. Let cool. Cream 1 C. Crisco and 1 C. white sugar. Add flour mixture and 1 t. vanilla and cream well. Then add 2 1/2 C. powdered sugar.

Mrs. Raymond D. Miller

Coffee Cake

1 egg, beaten
½ C. milk
2 t. baking powder
2 T. melted shortening

½ C. sugar
1 C. flour
½ t. salt

Combine egg, sugar, milk and shortening. Add flour, sifted with baking powder and salt. Mix well and pour into greased floured pan. Sprinkle with topping and bake at 350° for 20-25 minutes. Serves 8.

Topping

¼ C. brown sugar
1 T. flour

1 t. cinnamon
1 T. melted butter

Mrs. Henry E. Mast

Butter Pecan Cake

⅔ C. white sugar
1 C. brown sugar
3 eggs
¾ C. lard
3 t. baking powder
1¼ t. maple flavoring

¾ C. chopped nuts
2 C. flour
1 t. salt
1 t. vanilla
1 C. milk

Cream lard and sugars. Add eggs and remaining ingredients. Add flour last. Bake at 350° for 30 minutes.

Mrs. Henry E. Mast

1-2-3-4 Cake

1 C. oleo
2 C. sugar
3 C. flour
3 t. baking powder
½ t. salt

4 eggs
1 C. milk
1 t. vanilla
½ t. almond extract

Cream oleo and sugar, add eggs and remaining ingredients, adding flour last. Bake at 350° for 30 minutes or until golden brown.

Delicious Shortcake

1/2 C. sugar
6 T. oleo
1 egg
2 t. baking powder

3/4 t. salt
1 t. vanilla
1/2 C. milk
2 C. flour

Topping

4 T. white sugar
1 T. flour

1/2 t. cinnamon

Combine ingredients in order and put in pan. Put 1 1/2 T. melted butter over the top and then put topping on and bake at 375° for 25-30 minutes.

Mrs. J.L. Miller

Banana Nut Cake

Sift together in bowl:
2 1/2 C. cake flour
1 2/3 C. sugar
1 1/4 t. baking powder

1 1/4 t. soda
1 t. salt

Add:
2/3 C. shortening
1/3 C. buttermilk

1 1/4 C. mashed bananas (3)

Beat vigorously for 2 minutes then add:

1/3 C. buttermilk
2 eggs, unbeaten

Beat 2 minutes. Fold in:

2/3 C. chopped nuts

Pour batter into 2 round 9" x 1 1/2" prepared pans. Bake at 350° for 30-35 minutes.

Mrs. Henry E. Mast

24

Chiffon Cake

Grease and flour 13" x 9" oblong pan.

Sift together:

1³/₄ C. flour	³/₄ t. soda
1 C. sugar	1 t. salt

Add:

¹/₃ C. cooking oil	¹/₂ C. buttermilk

Add:

¹/₂ C. buttermilk	2 T. Nestles Quik or
2 egg yolks	chocolate chips

Beat one more minute. Fold in:

2 egg whites	¹/₂ C. sugar

Beat egg whites and sugar to a stiff meringue.

Mrs. Aden Chupp

Miracle Whip Cake

Sift into bowl:	Add:
2 C. all-purpose flour	1 t. vanilla
1 C. sugar	1 C. Miracle Whip (scant)
2 t. soda	1 C. cold water
4 T. cocoa	
¹/₂ t. salt	

Bake at 350° for 25-30 minutes.

Mary Ellen Troyer

*"God wisely designed the human body
so that we can neither pat our own backs
nor kick ourselves too easily."*

Amish Cake

Cream together:

1 stick oleo or ¼ lb. butter	1 lb. brown sugar

Add:

2 C. buttermilk or sour milk	2 t. soda

Add:

3 C. sifted flour	2 t. vanilla

Bake at 375°. Spread topping on and put back into oven for approximately one minute or until bubbly.

Topping

6 T. soft butter	1 C. brown sugar
4 T. milk	½ C. nuts (English walnuts)

Mrs. Henry E. Mast

Boston Cream Pie

1 box yellow cake mix
2 boxes vanilla instant pudding

Frosting

1 C. Nestles Quik	2¼ C. powdered sugar
⅓ C. boiling water	¼ C. oleo

Melt oleo in boiling water and Nestles Quik. Add powdered sugar and spread over cake.

*"The most important thing
a father can do for his children
is to love their mother."*

Crumb Cake

2 C. brown sugar
2 C. flour
1 stick butter
1 C. nuts
1 egg

1 t. soda
1 C. sour milk
1 t. vanilla
½ t. salt

Mix together first 4 ingredients to form crumbs. Set aside 1 C. of mixture. Combine remaining sugar mixture with rest of ingredients. Put in greased 9" x 13" pan and put 1 C. of crumb mixture over top. Bake at 325° for 45-55 minutes.

Mrs. David Hershberger

Zucchini Squash Cake

¼ C. soft oleo
½ C. vegetable oil
1¾ C. white sugar
2 eggs
1 t. vanilla
½ C. sour milk
2½ C. unsifted flour
4 T. cocoa

½ t. baking powder
1 t. soda
½ t. cinnamon
½ t. cloves
2 C. finely chopped zucchini
¼ C. chocolate chips
¼ C. chopped nuts

Mix all ingredients together except zucchini. Stir zucchini in last and pour in greased pan. Sprinkle with chocolate chips and nuts. Bake at 325° for 40-50 minutes.

Mrs. Dennis B. Miller

Hickory Nut Cake

2 C. white sugar
½ C. oleo
1 C. lukewarm water
3 C. flour plus 1 T.
  sifted flour

3 t. baking powder
5 egg whites
1 C. hickory nuts

Cream oleo and sugar. Add egg whites, baking powder and water. Then add flour and nuts. Bake at 350° for 30 minutes.

Mrs. Albert M. Yoder

Glazed Orange Cake

2 C. sifted flour
2½ t. baking powder
¼ t. soda
¼ t. salt
½ C. butter

1 C. sugar
½ C. walnuts
1 T. grated orange rind
2 eggs, beaten
¾ C. sour cream

Glaze

1 C. sugar

½ C. strained orange juice

Cream butter and sugar until fluffy. Add nuts, rind and eggs. Sift dry ingredients, alternating with sour cream. Mix well and put in greased 9" square pan. Bake at 375° for 40 minutes. Combine glaze ingredients and boil 5 minutes. Pour over hot cake.

Mary Esta Yoder

Banana Cake

2 C. white sugar
2 egg yolks
1 t. soda (scant)
3 t. baking powder
½ C. oleo

1 C. sweet milk
3 C. flour
3 bananas, mashed
2 egg whites, beaten stiff

Alternate dry ingredients with milk. Add bananas and beaten egg whites last and 1 t. vanilla. Bake at 350°.

Mrs. David E. Hershberger

Deep Dark Chocolate Cake

2 C. flour
2 C. sugar
½ C. cocoa
1½ t. soda
1½ t. baking powder
1 C. boiling water

1 t. salt
2 eggs
1 C. milk
½ C. vegetable oil
2 t. vanilla

Combine dry ingredients in large mixer bowl. Add eggs, milk, oil and vanilla. Stir in boiling water. Pour in greased pan. Bake at 350°.

Mrs. Albert A. Raber, Jr.

Cocoa Chiffon Cake

³/₄ C. boiling water
½ C. cocoa
1³/₄ C. sifted cake flour
1³/₄ C. sugar
3 t. baking powder
1 t. salt
½ C. cooking oil

7 unbeaten egg yolks
1 t. vanilla
¼ t. red food coloring
1 C. egg whites (7-8)
½ t. cream of tartar

Mix boiling water and cocoa, stir until smooth. Cool. Sift dry ingredients into a bowl. Make a well and add oil, egg yolks, cooled cocoa mixture, vanilla and coloring. Beat with spoon until smooth or with electric mixer 1 minute at medium speed. Beat egg whites and cream of tartar until whites form very stiff peaks. Pour into ungreased 9 inch square or 10" x 4" round tube pan. Bake at 350° for 55 minutes. Invert pan over neck of funnel or bottle.

Mary Ann N. Coblentz

Brownie Cake

Bring to boil:
2 sticks oleo
1 C. water
Remove from heat and add:
2 C. white sugar
½ t. salt
2 C. flour
2 eggs

4 T. cocoa

1 t. soda
1 t. baking powder
½ C. sour cream

Bake at 350°.

Brownie Icing

1 stick butter
4 T. cocoa

6 T. milk

Bring to boil and add 1 t. vanilla and powdered sugar as desired and chopped nuts. Mix and spread on cake as soon as cake is done.

Mrs. J.L. Miller

Pineapple Ice Box Cake

½ lb. vanilla wafers
2 C. powdered sugar
½ C. butter
1 large can crushed pineapple

2 eggs
½ pt. whipping cream
½ C. nuts

Crush wafers and put half in bottom of pan. Cream sugar and butter until fluffy. Add eggs. Put on top of crumbs. Then add a layer of drained pineapple. Add a layer of whipped cream and nuts mixed together and add remaining crumbs and place in refrigerator 12 hours before serving. Serves 10. (Whipped cream should be sweetened to taste, but if Rich's topping is used add no sugar.)

Mrs. Katie T. Hostetler

Ho Ho Cake

Mix and bake a chocolate cake mix. Cool.

Topping:
5 T. flour
1¼ C. milk
1 C. Crisco

1 C. white sugar
1 stick oleo

Cook flour and milk together until thick, stirring constantly. Cool completely. Cream the last 3 ingredients and gradually add to flour mixture. Beat well and spread over warm cake.

Frosting:
1 stick oleo
1 egg
1 t. vanilla

3 pkg. pre-melted chocolate
2½ T. hot water
3 C. powdered sugar

Melt oleo and combine with remaining ingredients and beat well. Spread over cake and refrigerate.

Lizzie Ann Erb

Favorite Coffee Cake

1½ C. flour
¾ C. sugar
¼ C. shortening
¾ C. milk

2½ t. baking powder
¾ t. salt
1 egg

Heat oven to 375°. Grease round pans. Blend above ingredients. Beat and spread in pans.

Topping

⅓ C. brown sugar
¼ C. flour

1½ t. cinnamon
3 T. oleo

Mix above ingredients until crumbly. Sprinkle over batter. Bake 25-30 minutes or until done.

Mrs. John A. Weaver

Black Midnight Cake

⅔ C. shortening
1⅔ C. white sugar
3 eggs
2¼ C. cake flour
⅔ C. cocoa

¼ t. baking powder
1¼ t. soda
1 t. salt
1⅓ C. water
1 t. vanilla

Bake in 2 layer pans or 1 oblong pan 40-45 minutes at 350°.

Cream Filling

2 egg whites, beaten stiffly
1 t. vanilla

2 C. powdered sugar

Beat well and add 1½ C. Crisco. Beat until smooth.

Mrs. Melvin E. Mast

Angel Food Cake

Sift together 3 times:
1¼ C. sifted cake flour
 Mix:
1¾ C. egg whites
1½ t. cream of tartar

2 C. white sugar

¼ t. salt

Beat egg whites, cream of tartar and salt till stiff. Fold in sugar and flour mixture. Add 2 t. vanilla. Bake at 300° for 1 hour or until done.

Mrs. Andy C. Yoder

Shawn's Cold Water Chocolate Cake

1 C. white sugar
1/2 C. shortening
2 C. flour
1 1/4 C. cold water
1/2 C. cocoa

1/2 t. salt
1/2 t. soda
2 T. hot water
3 egg whites
3/4 C. white sugar

Cream sugar and shortening. Add flour, cold water, cocoa and salt. Beat till smooth. Dissolve soda in hot water. Beat egg whites until stiff and add 3/4 C. white sugar. Fold into batter.

Topping

1 C. crushed graham crackers
1/4 C. melted butter or oleo
1 C. small chocolate chips

1/2 C. chopped nuts
1/8 t. salt

Mix and sprinkle over cake batter and bake at 350° for 30-35 minutes. (You can also use a cake mix and put the above chocolate crunch topping on.)

Mrs. Eli A. Beachy

Oatmeal Picnic Cake

1 C. instant oatmeal
1 C. boiling water

Mix and let stand for 20 minutes. Add:

1 C. white sugar
1 C. brown sugar
1/2 C. vegetable oil or
    melted shortening
1 1/3 C. sifted flour

1 t. soda
1 t. cinnamon
1 t. salt
2 eggs

Mix ingredients. Bake at 350° in a 9" x 13" pan.

Topping

1 C. brown sugar
2 T. butter

6 T. cream
1/2 C. coconut or nuts

Mix and put on hot cake and bake for a few more minutes.

Mary Ellen Troyer

32

Oatmeal Chocolate Cake

1³/₄ C. boiling water
1 C. uncooked oatmeal
1 C. brown sugar (packed)
1 C. white sugar
¹/₂ C. butter
2 large eggs

1³/₄ C. flour
1 t. soda
¹/₂ t. salt
1 T. cocoa
12 oz. chocolate chips
³/₄ C. nuts

Pour boiling water over oatmeal. Let stand 10 minutes. Add sugars and butter. Stir until butter is melted then add the next 5 ingredients. Add half of the chocolate chips. Pour in greased 9 x 13 inch pan. Sprinkle nuts and rest of chocolate chips on top. Bake at 350° for 40 minutes. Very good.

Edna Troyer

Very Good Chocolate Cake

¹/₂ C. shortening
1 C. white sugar
1 C. brown sugar
2 eggs
pinch of salt

2 C. boiling water
¹/₂ C. cocoa
2 t. soda
2 t. baking powder
2 C. flour

Mix in order. Batter will be thin. Bake at 350° for 38 minutes.

Ho Ho Frosting for Chocolate Cake

Filling
Cook 1¹/₄ C. milk with 5 T. flour until thick. Chill. Beat ¹/₂ C. oleo, 1 C. Crisco and 1 C. sugar until creamy. Add the chilled milk mixture and spread on cooled cake. Set aside.

Frosting

¹/₂ C. oleo, melted
4 oz. bar sweet chocolate
   or cocoa
1 egg

1 t. vanilla
3 C. powdered sugar
2¹/₂ T. water

Blend all ingredients until creamy and spread on top of cream filling. May be runny at first.

Mrs. Junior A. Yoder

Moist Angel Food Cake

1 C. cake flour
1½ C. powdered sugar
1½ C. egg whites
1½ t. vanilla

1½ t. cream of tartar
½ t. salt
1 C. granulated sugar

Measure and sift together flour and powdered sugar. Sift granulated sugar. Beat egg whites till peaks can be formed. Add cream of tartar, salt and vanilla. Fold in granulated sugar, then flour and sugar mixture. Bake at 350° for 40-50 minutes in angel food cake pan.

Optional: Use ⅓ C. cocoa and ⅔ C. flour instead of 1 C. flour, or use ⅓ C. or 1 small box jello and ⅔ C. granulated sugar instead of 1 C. granulated sugar.

Mrs. Aden J. Raber

Ho Ho Filling

Mix and bake a chocolate cake mix in sheet cake pan. Cool. Spread filling on cake. Let set then frost with frosting. Ho Ho cake recipe is found on page 30.

1¼ C. milk
    Cook till thick. Cool.

5 T. flour

1 stick oleo
1 C. white sugar
    Add to flour mixture and stir till fluffy.

½ C. Crisco

Frosting

3 C. powdered sugar
¾ C. cocoa
1 T. vanilla

1 stick oleo
1 egg, beaten
2½ T. hot water

Beat egg. Add oleo and soften. Add powdered sugar, cocoa and vanilla. Beat well. Add hot water. Mix and spread onto cake.

Ada J. Yoder

Sugarless Cake

1 C. hot water
½ C. Crisco
1 C. molasses
2¼ C. flour
¾ C. cocoa

2 eggs
2 t. soda
½ t. salt
1 t. vanilla

Mix all ingredients. Bake at 350° until golden brown.

Easy Fruitcake

Cream together:

½ C. shortening   1 stick oleo

Add:

1 C. sugar (add gradually)   2 eggs

Beat well and add 2 C. sifted flour gradually. Spread mixture in 13 x 9 inch greased pan, saving ½ C. of dough. Spread 1 can apple pie filling and top with drops of remaining dough and bake at 350° for 40 minutes. While cake is still warm spread with powdered sugar.

Mrs. Nelson A. Barkman

Pumpkin Cake

Beat together:

2 C. sugar   4 eggs, beaten

2 C. pumpkin   1 C. Wesson oil

Stir together and blend in:

2 C. Gold Medal flour   1 t. pumpkin pie spice

2 t. baking soda   2 t. cinnamon

2 t. baking powder   ½ t. salt

1 t. nutmeg

Fill 12 cupcake cups with batter. Pour remainder of batter in greased and floured cake pan. Bake at 350° for 30 minutes. Cool and ice.

Frosting

3 C. powdered sugar   8 oz. cream cheese

½ C. margarine, softened

Mrs. Reuben Miller

Sunday Spice Cake

2½ C. flour   2½ t. baking powder

1¼ C. brown sugar   1 t. cinnamon

⅔ C. Crisco   ½ t. cloves

⅓ C. Karo   ½ t. nutmeg

1⅓ C. milk   ½ t. allspice

3 eggs   1 t. salt

Cream together Crisco and brown sugar, add rest of ingredients. Bake at 350° until golden brown.

Kentucky Cream Cake

½ C. vegetable oil
1 stick margarine
2 C. sugar
5 egg yolks
2¼ C. flour
1 t. soda

1 C. buttermilk
1 t. vanilla
1 C. coconut
⅔ C. chopped nuts
5 egg whites, beaten

Cream oil and margarine with sugar. Add egg yolks one at a time. Beat well. Add flour and soda alternately with buttermilk. Add vanilla, coconut and nuts. Fold in egg whites. Bake in two or three 8" x 8" x 2" layers at 350° for 35-40 minutes. Spread frosting between layers and stack.

Mrs. Tobie W. Hostetler

Graham Streusel Cake

1 box yellow cake mix. Mix as directed on box.

Crumbs

2 C. graham crackers, crushed
¾ C. brown sugar
1 stick butter

¾ C. chopped nuts
1 t. cinnamon

Pour ½ of cake mix in pan. Sprinkle ½ of crumbs on top. Add remaining cake batter, then another layer of crumbs. Make a glaze of 1 C. powdered sugar and 1 or 2 T. water and drizzle on top of cake once it is cooled.

Mrs. Abe E. Mast

Crazy Chocolate Cake

2 C. white sugar
1 C. shortening
¾ C. cocoa
2 eggs
1 C. sour milk or buttermilk
2 t. soda

1 T. baking powder
1 t. vanilla
3 C. flour
1 C. boiling coffee
¼ t. salt

Cream white sugar and shortening. Add rest of ingredients, mix well. Bake at 350°.

Mrs. Albert A. Raber, Jr.

Carrot Cake

2 C. sugar
4 eggs
2 t. soda
2 t. baking powder
3 C. raw carrots,
  ground or shredded

1 1/2 C. cooking oil
2 C. flour
1 t. salt
1 t. cinnamon
1/2 C. chopped nuts

Cream sugar and cooking oil. Add eggs and beat well. Sift flour, soda, salt, baking powder and cinnamon together. Add the creamed mixture. Fold in carrots and nuts. Bake at 350° for 1 hour in a 9" x 13" pan or layer cake pan. Cool.

Cream Cheese Frosting

4 oz. cream cheese
1-1 1/2 C. powdered sugar
1 t. vanilla

1/2 stick oleo
1/4 C. chopped nuts

Soften cream cheese and oleo. Blend in powdered sugar and vanilla. Add chopped nuts.

Mrs. Viola Miller

Alaska Sheet Cake

2 sticks butter
  Put in saucepan and bring to a boil.

1 C. water

2 1/2 C. flour
2 C. white sugar
1/2 C. buttermilk

1 t. soda
1 t. salt
3 eggs

Measure dry ingredients into a bowl. Add butter and water mixture to dry ingredients, mix well. Add eggs and buttermilk. Bake in a large cookie sheet at 375° for 20 minutes.

Frosting

1/2 C. oleo

3 T. milk

Bring to a boil and add 1 lb. powdered sugar and 1 t. vanilla. Spread on cake while warm. Sprinkle coconut or nuts on top.

Mary Esta Yoder

Fluffy White Cake

Cream together until fluffy:
½ C. soft shortening (half butter)   1½ C. sugar

Sift together:
2½ C. flour   1 t. salt
2½ t. baking powder

Mix alternately with:
1 C. milk   1½ t. flavoring

Fold in:
4 egg whites

Bake at 350° for 35-40 minutes in a 9" x 13" pan.

Mrs. John A. Weaver

Angel Food Chocolate Cake

2 C. white sugar   2 t. vanilla
2 C. egg whites   1 C. plus 5 T. cake flour
2 t. cream of tartar   3 T. cocoa
½ t. salt

Put egg whites, cream of tartar and salt in large mixing bowl and beat at medium speed until foamy. Add 1 C. sugar, 2 T. at a time into the foamy egg whites while beating at medium speed. After last sugar is added, beat on high until stiff. Fold in vanilla. Sift together remaining sugar, flour and cocoa. Add to egg whites in 3 parts. After each addition fold in gently with wire whip, 25 whips for each addition. Bake at 375° for 40-45 minutes in angel food cake pan. For white cake use 1½ C. cake flour and omit cocoa.

Mary Ann Coblentz

Quick Cocoa Cake

3 C. flour   1 t. salt
2 C. brown sugar   1¾ C. warm water
5 T. Nestles Quik cocoa   1¼ C. vegetable oil
2 t. soda   4 eggs
2 t. baking powder

Mix and beat well. Bake at 350° for 45 minutes.

Mrs. Henry J.C. Yoder

Mocha Oatmeal Chocolate Chip Cake

1³/₄ C. boiling water
1 C. quick oatmeal
1 T. instant coffee
1 C. brown sugar
¹/₂ C. butter or oleo
³/₄ C. white sugar
2 eggs

1³/₄ C. flour
1 t. soda
¹/₂ t. salt
1 T. cocoa
1 pkg. chocolate chips
   (12 oz.)
³/₄ C. chopped nuts

Pour boiling water over oatmeal and coffee. Let stand at room temperature for 10 minutes. Add sugars and oleo and stir till oleo melts. Add eggs, mix well. Sift dry ingredients and add to sugar mixture. Mix well, add half of the chocolate chips. Pour batter into greased 9" x 13" pan. Sprinkle nuts and remaining chips on top. Bake at 350° for 40 minutes or until done. Let cool then drizzle with glaze.

Glaze

2 T. hot water   ¹/₂ t. instant coffee
1¹/₂ C. powdered sugar

Mix together and drizzle over cooled cake.

Mary Esta Yoder

Watergate Cake

1 box white cake mix
1 C. plus 1 T. vegetable oil
1 box pistachio instant pudding mix
¹/₂ C. chopped pecans
1 C. ginger ale
3 eggs

Put in greased and floured 9" x 13" pan. Bake at 350° for 30 minutes. Cool and add topping when ready to serve.

Topping

8 oz. Cool Whip or 2 C. Rich's topping
³/₄ C. milk
1 pkg. pistachio instant pudding

Mix and pour over cake, let set. Very good.

Mrs. Eli A. Beachy

Chocolate Chip Chiffon Cake

Step 1:

2¼ C. cake flour
1¾ C. white sugar
   Measure and sift together in bowl.

3 t. baking powder
1 t. salt

⅓ C. salad oil
5 unbeaten egg yolks
   Add to dry ingredients. Beat until smooth.

¾ C. cold water
2 t. vanilla

Step 2:

1 C. egg whites (7 or 8)   ½ t. cream of tartar

Whip until whites form very stiff peaks. They should be much stiffer than for angel food cake. Do not underbeat.

Step 3:

Pour egg mixture gradually over whipped egg whites, gently folding with spatula till blended. Do not stir. Sprinkle 3 oz. coarsely grated chocolate over top of batter, gently folding in with a few strokes. Pour into 10" ungreased tube pan. Bake at 325° for 55 minutes then at 350° for 10-15 minutes, or bake in 9" x 13" pan at 350° for 45-50 minutes.

Mrs. David D. Miller

Angel Food Cake Deluxe

1 C. cake flour
1½ C. powdered sugar
1½ C. egg whites (approx. 12)
1½ t. cream of tartar

1 C. white sugar
¼ t. salt
1½ t. vanilla

Mix flour and powdered sugar. Beat egg whites and cream of tartar until foamy. Beat in sugar 2 T. at a time. Continue beating until stiff and glossy. Add salt and vanilla. Do not underbeat. Sprinkle flour and powdered sugar mixture ¼ C. at a time, folding in just until mixture disappears. Bake at 350°-375° for 30-35 minutes. Turn upside down until cool.

Mrs. Roman E. Raber

Chocolate Cake

2 C. white sugar	2 t. soda
3 C. flour	1/2 t. salt
2 t. baking powder	

Mix above ingredients in a bowl and make a well. Add:

2 eggs, beaten	1/2 C. butter, lard or
1 C. sour milk or buttermilk	shortening

Mix and add:

1 C. water and 1/2 C. cocoa, boiled together
1 t. vanilla

Bake at 350° in a large loaf pan. This is a very moist cake.

Mrs. Jonas A.M. Yoder

Spiced Apple Cake

Sift:

1 C. brown sugar	1 t. baking powder
2 C. all-purpose flour	1 t. soda
1/4 t. salt	

Add: 1/2 C. shortening to make crumbs.

Then add:

1 egg	1 t. vanilla
1/2 C. milk	

Mix well. Add 4 or 5 diced apples. Pour into well greased pan.

Topping

3 T. melted butter	1 t. cinnamon
1 C. brown sugar	1 C. chopped nuts
1/2 C. flour	

Spread over the top and bake at 350° for 45 minutes.

Mrs. Dan A. Nisley

Graham Streusel Cake

Crumbs:

2 C. graham cracker crumbs

1 1/4 t. cinnamon

3/4 C. packed brown sugar

3/4 C. oleo, melted

Mix:

1 pkg. moist yellow cake mix

1/3 C. vegetable oil

1 C. water

3 eggs

Pour 2 1/3 C. batter into greased pan. Sprinkle with 2 C. crumbs. Pour remaining batter into pan. Sprinkle with remaining crumbs. Bake for 45-50 minutes or until cake is done. Cool, drizzle with glaze.

Glaze

1 C. powdered sugar

1 T. water

Mix, stir in additional water, one teaspoon at a time, until smooth and of desired consistency.

Mrs. Elmer Yoder

Large Chocolate Cake

2 C. white sugar

3/4 C. shortening

2 eggs, beaten

2 1/2 C. flour

1/2 C. cocoa

1 C. sour milk or buttermilk

1 t. vanilla

1/2 t. salt

2 t. soda

1 C. boiling water

Cream shortening, sugar and eggs. Mix well. Add alternately the flour sifted with cocoa and sour milk. Mix carefully. Add salt and vanilla. Dissolve soda in boiling water and add to mixture. Bake at 350° for 30 minutes in a 9" x 13" cake pan.

Mrs. Daniel Barkman

Sponge Roll

4 eggs	1 C. sifted cake flour
1 t. vanilla	¾ t. baking powder
1 C. white sugar	¼ t. salt

Beat eggs and vanilla at high speed until thick and lemon colored. Gradually beat in sugar until mixture is fluffy and thick. Sift together the dry ingredients and add to egg mixture. Do not beat. Bake in jelly roll pan at 375° for 6-8 minutes.

Filling

8 T. flour (level)	⅔ C. hot water
1 C. brown sugar	1 stick butter
maple or vanilla flavoring	

Cook flour, brown sugar and hot water together then add butter and flavoring. Cool. Spread on cake while hot and roll like jelly roll.

Mrs. Emanuel Weaver

Moist Apple Cake

3 eggs	1 t. salt
1¼ C. white sugar	1 t. cinnamon
1 C. salad oil	2 C. chopped apples
2 C. flour	1 C. chopped nuts (optional)
1 t. soda	

Beat eggs, sugar and oil. Sift in dry ingredients. Fold in apples and nuts. Bake at 350° for 40-50 minutes in a 9" x 13" pan.

Mrs. Levi Beachy

Jelly Roll

4 eggs   ¼ t. salt
¾ t. baking powder
   Beat until foamy. Add:
¾ C. white sugar (1 T. at a time)
   Beat until thick and lemon colored. Fold in:
¾ C. cake flour

   Bake at 400° for 6-8 minutes on a 10" x 15" cookie sheet.

Filling

5 T. butter   1 C. brown sugar
   Heat above until slightly browned and add:
1 C. hot water   1 t. vanilla
7 T. flour (level)

   Let cool and spread on jelly roll as soon as it comes out of the oven and roll up.

Mrs. Roman E. Raber

Jelly Roll

1 C. cake flour   1 C. white sugar
1 t. baking powder   ⅓ C. water
¼ t. salt   1 t. vanilla
3 eggs

   Beat eggs till lemon colored. Beat in sugar, water and vanilla. Add dry ingredients. Beat until batter is smooth. Remove from pan and roll in wet towel.

Filling

2 C. powdered sugar   8 oz. Cool Whip
8 oz. cream cheese

   This makes enough filling for two jelly rolls.

Mrs. Adam Yoder

Old-Fashioned Jelly Roll

³/₄ C. sifted cake flour
³/₄ t. baking powder
¹/₄ t. salt

4 eggs
1 t. vanilla
³/₄ C. sugar

Sift flour once, combine baking powder, salt and eggs in bowl. Place over smaller bowl of hot water. Beat, adding sugar gradually until mixture is thick and light colored. Remove bowl from hot water. Fold in flour and vanilla. Pour in 15" x 10" pan lined with wax paper and greased and floured. Bake at 400° for 13 minutes. Let cool a little. Remove from pan on cloth or wax paper covered with powdered sugar. Remove paper, spread filling. Roll quickly. Wrap in cloth and put on rack till cold.

For filling: I usually cook butterscotch same as for pie or make a clear jel sauce and add jello. Use your favorite jello for flavor.

Mrs. Ura J. Miller

Jelly Roll

3 eggs
1 C. white sugar
¹/₃ C. water
1 t. vanilla

1 C. Softasilk flour
1 t. baking powder
¹/₄ t. salt

Beat eggs. Add rest of ingredients and mix. (Add 2 T. cocoa to make a chocolate jelly roll.)

Filling

2¹/₃ C. powdered sugar
¹/₄ t. salt
1 egg white, beaten

1 t. vanilla
¹/₂ C. Crisco

Boil 2 T. water and ¹/₄ C. white sugar for 1 minute. Cool and mix with rest of ingredients.

Mrs. Eli A. Yoder

Texas Sheet Cake Icing

Bring to boil:
1 stick oleo   6 T. milk
4 t. cocoa

Add:
2 C. powdered sugar   1 C. walnuts
1 t. vanilla

Spread while hot.

Mrs. Aden J. Raber

Frosting

8 oz. cream cheese   1 t. vanilla
½ stick margarine   chopped nuts
1 lb. powdered sugar

Cream first four ingredients together. Frost cake. Top with nuts.

Mrs. Tobie W. Hostetler

Angel Food Cake Icing

1½ C. milk   2 eggs, well beaten
½ C. white sugar   ¼ t. salt
3 T. cold water   2 pkg. gelatine
whipped topping (enough to make nice and fluffy)

Mix together milk, beaten eggs, sugar and salt. Put on low heat. Stir until it lightly coats the spoon. Don't overcook. Soften gelatine in cold water and add to custard. Cool till partly thick and fold in whipped topping. When thick enough to spread, frost cake. Add food coloring for colored icing if desired.

Mrs. J.L. Miller

Quick Caramel Icing

6 T. butter   ¾ C. brown sugar
6 T. milk   2 C. powdered sugar

Mix brown sugar and butter and blend. Add milk and just bring to a boiling point. Remove from heat and gradually add powdered sugar.

Mrs. Dan Erb

- *Favorite Recipes* -

- *Notes* -

Cookies

Oatmeal Chip Cookies

³/₄ C. butter
1¹/₄ C. brown sugar
2 eggs
2 C. flour
2 t. cream of tartar
1 t. soda

¹/₂ t. salt
1 C. oatmeal
1 C. nuts
1 C. chocolate chips
1 C. butterscotch chips

Mix butter and sugar together. Add eggs and dry ingredients. Add oatmeal, nuts and chips last. Drop by teaspoon on greased cookie sheet. Bake at 400°.

Mrs. David E. Hershberger

Date Cookies

1 C. shortening
2 C. brown sugar
3 eggs, beaten

4 C. flour
¹/₄ t. salt
¹/₂ t. soda

Chill for 2 hours. Roll out and cut.

Filling

2¹/₄ C. dates
1 C. white sugar

1 C. water

Boil till mixture is thick and then add 1 C. nuts. Chill. Sandwich ¹/₂ - 1 t. filling between two cookies before baking. Bake at 400°.

Lizzie Raber

Christmas Cookies

6 C. flour
1 T. baking soda
1 t. salt
1 t. ginger
1 t. cinnamon

1³/₄ C. shortening
1 C. boiling water
1 C. molasses
1 C. sugar

Sift flour, soda, salt and spices. Combine remaining ingredients. Add flour mixture. Chill and roll dough on floured pastry sheet. Cut with cookie cutter. Bake at 375° for 12 minutes.

Mrs. David R. Yoder

Chocolate Chip Cookies

1 C. soft shortening
1/2 C. white sugar
1/2 C. brown sugar
2 eggs
8 oz. pkg. chocolate chips

2 3/4 C. sifted flour
1/2 t. soda
1 t. salt
1 1/2 t. vanilla

Mix sugar, shortening and beaten eggs together. Add flour, soda and salt. Last add vanilla and chocolate chips. Bake at 400°.

Fannie Miller

Orange Drop Cookies

2/3 C. shortening
3/4 C. sugar
1 egg
1/2 C. orange juice

2 C. flour
1/2 t. baking powder
1/2 t. soda
1/2 t. salt

Cream shortening and sugar. Add egg. Blend. Add orange juice, baking powder, soda and salt. Beat well. Then add flour. Bake at 400°. Makes 4 dozen cookies.

Orange Butter Icing

2 C. powdered sugar
2 T. butter

2 T. orange juice

Blend together and spread onto cookies.

Mrs. Albert A. Raber, Jr.

Peanut Butter Squares

1/2 C. white sugar
1/2 C. brown sugar
1 egg
1/2 C. oleo or butter
1/3 C. peanut butter

1 C. flour
1 C. quick oats
1/2 t. soda
1/4 t. salt

Cream sugars, oleo or butter and peanut butter, then add remaining ingredients. Bake at 350° until golden brown. Bake in cookie sheet.

Peanut Butter Frosting

1 1/2 C. powdered sugar
1/4 C. peanut butter

2 T. milk

Reserve 1/3 C. of peanut butter frosting, mix with 3 T. cocoa and 1 T. milk. Spread both frostings on cookies. Cut in bars.

Mrs. Albert A. Raber, Jr.

Chocolate Marshmallow Bars

½ C. oleo
1 C. brown sugar
1 egg
1 t. vanilla
¼ C. cocoa

2 C. flour
½ t. soda
½ t. salt
½ C. milk

Combine sugar, oleo, egg and vanilla. Add dry ingredients. Add milk. Spread on greased cookie sheet. Bake at 375° for 8 minutes. Remove from oven and sprinkle miniature marshmallows over top. Return to oven for 1 minute.

Icing

⅓ C. butter
1 C. brown sugar

2 T. cocoa
¼ C. milk

Combine and boil till it forms large bubbles. Cool and add powdered sugar. Spread thinly over cookies.

Mrs. Levi H. Mast

Raisin Top Cookies

2 C. brown sugar
2 eggs
1 T. vanilla
¼ t. salt

1 C. shortening
¼ C. milk
1 t. soda
4 C. all-purpose flour

Cream together sugar and shortening then add remaining ingredients. Roll dough in balls and place on cookie sheet. Make a little well to put in filling. Approximately 1 t. per cookie. Bake at 375°.

Filling

1 C. raisins, ground
¾ C. brown sugar

1 C. water
¼ t. salt

Cook then thicken with clear jel. Add maple flavoring.

Mary Yoder
Mrs. Eli D. Miller

Yummy Chocolate Chip Cookies

Cream together:

1 C. white sugar
1 C. brown sugar

1 C. oleo
2 eggs

Sift together:

2 C. flour
1 t. soda

1/2 t. salt
1/2 t. baking powder

Mix with first part and add:

1 t. vanilla
2 C. oatmeal

1 C. chocolate chips
1 C. chopped nuts

Drop by spoonfuls on ungreased cookie sheet. Bake at 350° for 8 minutes.

Mrs. Joe H. Bowman

Buttermilk Cookies

3-4 C. buttermilk
4 C. white sugar
4 C. brown sugar
3 C. butter or lard
12 eggs, beaten

8 t. soda
8 t. baking powder
2 t. salt
1 t. vanilla
14-16 C. flour

Cream sugars and butter or lard, add remaining ingredients. Add enough flour to make the dough firm enough to be dipped or rolled. Bake at 375°.

Mary Ellen Troyer

No-Bake Cookies

2 C. white sugar
3 T. cocoa
Boil 1 minute. Remove and add:
3 C. rolled oats
1/2 C. peanut butter

1/4 C. butter or oleo
1/2 C. milk

1 t. vanilla

Drop quickly by teaspoon on wax paper. Cool and serve.

Mrs. William Kuhns

California Coconut Date Cookies

1/2 C. butter or margarine
1/2 C. light brown sugar
1 1/4 C. all-purpose flour
2 eggs
1/2 t. vanilla
1/4 t. almond extract
1 can (3 1/2 oz.) shredded coconut
2/3 C. chopped dates
1/2 C. chopped blanched almonds or other kind of nut
1/4 C. all-purpose flour
2/3 C. light brown sugar

Using a mixer, cream butter. Add 1/2 C. brown sugar and mix until smooth. Gradually add 1 1/4 C. flour to form a smooth stiff dough. Place in an ungreased 13" x 9" x 2" oblong pan. Spread with fingers so it lines the pan evenly. Bake in preheated 350° oven for 15 minutes.

Meanwhile in another bowl, beat eggs slightly. Add the remaining ingredients in the order given. Mix after each addition. Spoon on top of mixture in pan; spread evenly. Return to oven for an additional 15 minutes or until edges become brown. Remove from oven and allow to cool. Cut cookie dough in half crosswise. Lift each half with a spatula and place on a cutting board. Cut into 2 inch squares. Store in an airtight container. Yield: 2-2 1/2 dozen. (Reduce oven temperature to 325° when using Baker's Secret bakeware.)

Mrs. Henry E. Mast

Butterscotch Crunch Cookies

4 C. margarine, softened
7 C. brown sugar
4 t. vanilla
8 eggs

6 C. all-purpose flour
4 t. soda
1 t. salt
12 C. oatmeal

Cream margarine and sugar. Add eggs. Beat well. Add rest of ingredients. Add oatmeal and flour last. Mix well. Bake at 350°. Do not overbake.

Mrs. David L. Troyer

Peanut Butter Oatmeal Bars

Cream well:
1/2 C. butter
1/2 C. white sugar

1/2 C. brown sugar

Add:
1 egg
1/3 C. peanut butter
1/4 t. salt

1/2 t. soda
1/2 t. vanilla

Add:
1 C. flour

1 C. quick rolled oats

Bake in a greased 13" x 9" pan at 350° for 20-25 minutes. Be careful not to overbake. After removing from oven immediately sprinkle with 1 C. chocolate chips.

Then mix together 1/2 C. powdered sugar, 1/2 C. peanut butter and 2-4 T. milk. When chocolate chips are melted spread them and drizzle peanut butter mixture on top and swirl. Let cool before cutting in bars.

Mrs. Mervin Lehman
Mrs. William Kuhns

Chocolate Chip Cookies

2 C. oleo
1 1/2 C. brown sugar
1 1/2 C. white sugar
4 eggs, beaten
2 t. vanilla
1 t. water

2 C. chocolate chips
1 1/2 C. nuts
2 t. soda
2 t. salt
5 C. flour

Cream sugars and oleo, add remaining ingredients. Drop by teaspoon onto greased baking sheet. Bake at 350°. Do not overbake.

Mrs. Merlin Troyer
Mrs. Henry M. Troyer

Lemon Blossom Sugar Cookies

3 C. white sugar
1½ C. oleo
6 eggs
pinch of salt

4 T. lemon flavoring
4 t. baking powder
7 C. Robin Hood flour
yellow food coloring

Cream sugar and oleo, add remaining ingredients. Cut with cutter shaped like a blossom. Take thimble and make a hole in center of blossom. Mix some white sugar and yellow food coloring then sprinkle on cookies before baking. Bake at 250°.

Susie Hershberger

Brown Sugar Cookies

4 C. brown sugar
2 C. oleo
7 C. flour, unsifted
4 t. baking powder
1 t. vanilla

6 eggs
2 t. soda
¼ t. salt
1 C. milk

Cream oleo and brown sugar together. Add eggs and mix well. Add milk and vanilla, mix. Last, add dry ingredients. Bake at 400°.

Mrs. Jonas J.D. Miller

Fudge Brownies

1½ C. Bisquick
½ C. white sugar
½-1 C. chopped nuts
½ C. milk

½ C. brown sugar (packed)
1¾ C. boiling water
3 T. cocoa

Mix together. Bake at 350° in a 9" x 13" pan. Serve warm with ice cream.

Mrs. Dennis B. Miller

Date Oatmeal Cookies

1³/₄ C. shortening
1 C. white sugar
1 C. brown sugar
4 eggs
1 C. buttermilk
2 t. soda

2 t. baking powder
2 t. salt
2 t. cinnamon
4 C. oatmeal
4 C. flour
1-1½ lb. dates

Cook dates in 1½ C. water. Cream together sugars and shortening. Add remaining ingredients including cooled dates. Drop by teaspoon on lightly greased baking sheet. Bake at 350°. Add nuts if desired.

Caramel Frosting

1 stick butter, melted
1 C. brown sugar

¼ t. salt

Cook this on low heat for 2 minutes, stirring constantly. Add ¼ C. milk or cream. Remove from heat and add powdered sugar as desired. Add vanilla and maple flavoring for taste.

Mrs. J.L. Miller

Poor Man's Cookies

Stir 1 C. raisins in 1½ C. water. (If not enough juice to fill 1 C. add water to make 1 C.) Add 2 T. Crisco and cool.

1 C. sugar
2 C. flour
½ t. nutmeg

1 t. soda
1 t. baking powder
1 t. cinnamon

Sift and add to raisin mixture. Spread on cookie sheet. Bake for 18-20 minutes.

Frosting

1 C. powdered sugar
hot water

1 T. butter

Mix and spread over bars while hot.

Mrs. William Kuhns

Frosted Cream Bars

1 C. shortening
1 C. sugar
1 C. dark molasses
4 C. flour (or less)
$1/2$ t. salt
$1^1/_2$ t. soda

2 eggs
1 C. sour milk or buttermilk
1 t. cinnamon
$1/2$ t. nutmeg
1 C. nuts

Cream sugar and shortening then add remaining ingredients. Mix and spread dough in thin layer on greased cookie sheet. Bake at 350° for 20-25 minutes. Frost with your favorite frosting. A good spicy cookie.

Cream Wafer Cookies

$1/2$ C. butter
1 C. brown sugar
2 eggs, beaten
1 t. vanilla

2 T. sweet cream
$1^1/_2$ t. soda
$2^3/_4$ C. flour

Cream together butter and sugar. Add remaining ingredients. Roll out dough thinner than for common cookies. Cut and bake at 350°. If you prefer chocolate cookies add 2 squares bitter chocolate to dough.

Filling

4 T. butter
1-2 T. hot sweet cream

2 C. powdered sugar
1 t. vanilla

Put filling between 2 cookies after baking cookies.

Sour Cream Cookies

1 C. brown sugar
1 C. white sugar
$4^1/_2$ C. flour
1 C. sour cream

$1/2$ C. shortening
3 t. baking powder
1 t. soda
2 eggs

Cream sugars and shortening. Add rest of ingredients. Drop by teaspoon on lightly greased cookie sheet. Bake at 350°.

Mrs. Henry E. Mast

Ranger Cookies

1 C. white sugar
1 C. brown sugar
1 C. shortening
2 C. flour

1 t. soda
1/2 t. baking powder
1/2 t. salt
2 eggs

Cream sugars and shortening until fluffy. Add beaten eggs. Mix well. Add flour, baking powder, soda and salt. Then add 2 C. rolled oats, 2 C. Rice Krispies and 1 C. coconut. Mix well. Drop by teaspoon on floured cookie sheet. Bake at 400°.

Mrs. Jonas N. Borntrager

Honey Delights

1 C. butter
2 C. honey or cane molasses
2 eggs
1/2 t. cinnamon
1/2 t. cloves

1/2 t. allspice
4 t. soda (wet in honey)
2 t. vanilla
8 C. flour (approx.)

Boil honey and butter together 1 minute. Cool. Add rest of ingredients and roll out 3/8" thick and cut in slices. Bake at 350°.

Mrs. Dan M. Miller

Prizewinning Cookies

4 C. brown sugar
2 C. shortening
2 C. sweet milk
4 eggs, well beaten

4 t. soda
10 t. baking powder
2 t. salt
2 t. vanilla

Cream sugar and shortening. Add remaining ingredients. Add flour as needed (approx. 7 C.) to drop. Bake at 350°. Frost with Crisco frosting.

Mrs. Edwin M. Troyer

Spicy Cookies

1 C. lard
2 C. brown sugar
1 C. plus 4 T. milk
3 eggs, beaten
2 t. baking powder
2 t. soda

1 t. cinnamon
½ t. cloves
1 t. vanilla
4 C. flour
1 C. chopped nuts

Cream sugar and lard. Add milk and beaten eggs then add remaining ingredients. Drop by teaspoon onto lightly greased cookie sheet.

Icing

6 T. butter, browned
3 T. hot water

1 t. vanilla

Add powdered sugar to spreading consistency.

Mrs. Henry E. Mast

Whoopie Pie Cookies

1½ C. lard
3 C. sugar
3 t. soda
1½ C. buttermilk
6 C. flour

1½ C. hot water
3 eggs
¾ C. cocoa
3 t. vanilla
3 t. salt

Cream together lard and sugar. Add soda to buttermilk. Add remaining ingredients. Drop on cookie sheet and bake at 350°.

Filling

3 egg whites
3 t. vanilla
1½ C. Crisco

5 T. milk
3 C. powdered sugar

Beat egg whites till stiff. Mix milk, powdered sugar, vanilla and Crisco. Add egg whites. Put filling between cookies like a sandwich.

Mrs. Henry E. Mast

Coconut Oatmeal Cookies

Cream:
2 C. shortening
2 C. brown sugar

2 C. white sugar

Then add:
4 eggs
5 C. oatmeal
2 C. coconut
3½ C. flour
2 t. soda

2 t. baking powder
2 t. vanilla
1 C. nuts
1 pkg. chocolate chips

Shape into rolls 1" thick and chill. Cut in ¼" slices and bake at 350°.

Everything Cookies

1 C. oleo
1 C. brown sugar
1 C. white sugar
1 egg
1 t. cream of tartar
1 t. salt (scant)
1 t. soda

1 C. quick oatmeal
1 C. coconut
1 C. salad oil
2 T. vanilla
3 C. flour
1 C. Rice Krispies
12 oz. pkg. chocolate chips

Mix in order given. Drop onto ungreased cookie sheet. Bake at 350° until lightly browned (cannot be tested like other cookies). If the dough is chilled, balls can be rolled by hand.

Mrs. Tobe Y. Hostetler

Pumpkin Bars

4 eggs
1²/₃ C. sugar
1 C. oil
16 oz. can or 2 C. pumpkin,
    drained

2 C. flour
1 t. soda
1 t. salt
2 t. baking powder
2 t. cinnamon

Combine eggs, sugar, oil and pumpkin. Beat until light. Add rest of ingredients and mix. Bake in 15" x 10" x 1" pan at 350° for 25-30 minutes. Cool and frost.

Frosting

3 oz. pkg. cream cheese, softened
1 t. vanilla

¹/₂ C. butter, softened
2 C. powdered sugar

Cream well and put on bars.

Mary Ann N. Coblentz
Mrs. Levi A. Hershberger
Mrs Mart R. Miller

Toll House Marble Squares

1 C. plus 2 T. flour
1/2 t. soda
1/2 t. salt
1/2 C. soft oleo
6 T. white sugar
6 T. brown sugar

1/2 t. vanilla
1/4 t. water
6 oz. pkg. chocolate chips
1/2 C. chopped nuts
1 egg

Sift together flour, soda and salt. Blend together oleo, sugars, vanilla and water. Beat in egg, add nuts. Mix in flour mixture. Spread in greased 9" x 13" pan. Sprinkle chocolate chips over dough. Place in oven 1 minute. Run knife through dough to marbleize. Bake at 375° for 12-14 minutes. Cool and cut.

Clara Yoder
Mrs. Mervin Lehman

Frosted Pumpkin Bars

4 eggs
1 C. salad oil
1 C. pumpkin
2 C. sugar
1/2 t. salt

2 t. cinnamon
1 t. baking powder
1/2 - 1 C. nuts
2 C. flour

Mix together and bake at 350° for 20 minutes on floured cookie sheet.

Frosting

8 oz. cream cheese
6 T. butter, melted
1 T. milk

3 1/2 C. powdered sugar
1 t. vanilla

Mix together and spread on while warm. Cut in squares.

Clara Yoder
Mrs. Ben D. Troyer
Lizzie Raber
Katie N. Troyer
Mrs. Henry M. Troyer
Mrs. David E. Hershberger

1-2-3 Coffee Bars

2²/₃ C. brown sugar
1 C. Wesson oil
1 C. coffee (use ½ t.
   instant coffee)
1 t. salt

1 t. soda
1 t. vanilla
2 eggs
3 C. flour

Mix well and pour in jelly roll pan. Put chocolate or butterscotch chips on the top. Sprinkle with chopped nuts. Bake at 300° for 25-30 minutes.

Mrs. Jonas J.D. Miller
Emma Hershberger
Edna Troyer
Ada Weaver

Brown Sugar Cookies

Cream together:
2 C. brown sugar
1 C. oleo

Then add:
3 eggs
1 t. vanilla
1 t. baking soda
2 T. hot water

4½ C. flour
1 t. baking powder
   (heaping)
1 t. salt

Dissolve soda in hot water. Mix all ingredients and chill overnight. Roll out, cut and bake at 375°. Put filling between two cookies after baking.

Filling

4 C. powdered sugar
8 oz. cream cheese

5 T. butter, softened

Mix together and add milk as needed.

Mrs. Roman E. Raber

Fudge Nut Bars

2 C. butter or oleo
4 C. brown sugar
4 eggs
4 t. vanilla

5 C. flour
2 t. soda
2 t. salt
6 C. quick oats

Cream together butter and sugar. Add eggs and vanilla. Stir in flour, soda, salt and oats. Set aside while making filling.

Filling

1 pkg. chocolate chips
1 can Eagle Brand milk
1 C. nuts

2 T. oleo
1 t. salt
2 t. vanilla

In saucepan over boiling water, mix together chocolate chips, milk, oleo and salt. Stir until smooth. Stir in nuts and vanilla. Spread a thin layer of oatmeal mixture over 2 cookie sheets. Add filling and remaining oatmeal mixture on top. Bake at 350° for 20 minutes or until lightly browned. Do not overbake.

Mrs. Mose M.E. Yoder
Fannie Troyer

Chocolate Cookies

2 C. brown sugar
1 C. shortening
1 C. milk
1 t. soda
2 eggs

3 C. flour, unsifted
2 t. baking powder
3/4 C. cocoa
1/4 t. salt
1 t. vanilla

Cream together sugar and shortening. Mix rest of ingredients in order given. Drop on cookie sheet and bake at 375°.

Mrs. Dennis B. Miller

Butterscotch Krispies

4 C. Robin Hood flour
3 C. brown sugar
4 C. rolled oats
2 C. soft shortening
4 eggs

2 t. vanilla
1 t. salt
1 t. soda
12 oz. butterscotch
chips

Drop by teaspoon onto cookie sheet and bake at 350°.

Mrs. Jonas N. Borntrager

Oreo Cookies

1 cake mix (white or chocolate)
2 eggs
2 T. water

2 T. cooking oil
½ C. cocoa

Let stand 20 minutes. Do not refrigerate. Shape in balls. Flatten with bottom of glass greased once and dipped into Nestles Quik for each cookie. Bake at 300° for 8 minutes.

Filling

1 envelope Knox gelatine
¼ C. cold water
1 T. plus 1 C. powdered sugar

1 t. vanilla
½ C. Crisco

Dissolve gelatine in cold water. Blend Crisco, powdered sugar and vanilla. Add gelatine. Mix and spread between 2 cookies.

Lizzie Ann Erb

Coffee Bars

2⅔ C. brown sugar
1 C. cooking oil
1 C. warm coffee (1 t. instant)
1 t. salt
1 t. vanilla

2 eggs
1 t. soda
1 C. nuts
3 C. flour

Mix everything in bowl and beat well. Spread on greased cookie sheet. Top with 1 C. chocolate chips. Bake at 350° for 25-30 minutes.

Lizzie Ann Erb

Jello Cookies

2¾ C. flour
1 t. soda
½ C. butter
½ t. almond flavoring/extract
½ t. salt

½ C. milk
½ C. white sugar
2 eggs
1 t. vanilla
3 oz. pkg. jello (dry)
(any flavor)

Cream butter and sugar, add eggs. Add remaining ingredients, adding flour last. Frost with powdered sugar frosting, same flavor as cookies.

Mary Yoder
Mrs. Emanuel Yoder

Pumpkin Bars

4 eggs	2 t. soda
1 C. salad oil	2 C. flour
2 C. pumpkin	2 t. cinnamon
2 C. white sugar	pinch of salt

Beat eggs. Add sugar, salad oil, pumpkin, salt, soda and cinnamon. Beat well then add flour. Bake at 350°.

Frosting

8 oz. cream cheese	1 t. vanilla
1 stick oleo	1 lb. powdered sugar

Soften cream cheese and oleo. Cream with powdered sugar and vanilla. Spread on cooled bars.

Mrs. Jonas J.D. Miller

Chocolate Bars

½ C. oleo	¼ t. baking powder
¾ C. white sugar	pinch of salt
2 eggs	1 t. vanilla
2 T. cocoa	nuts (optional)
¾ C. flour	

Cream together oleo and sugar. Add remaining ingredients. Spread out on cookie sheet. Bake at 350°. Do not bake more than 20 minutes. Then put 2-3 C. miniature marshmallows on top. Bake till they are melted. In saucepan melt 6 oz. pkg. chocolate chips and 1 C. peanut butter then add 1½ C. Rice Krispies. Spread on cooled bars.

Mrs. Reuben Miller

Christmas Logs

2 C. flour	1 C. oleo
½ C. powdered sugar	1 t. vanilla
½ t. salt	½ C. nuts
1 C. oatmeal	

Mix like pie crust and form in 3" logs. Bake at 375° till lightly browned. Frost and decorate.

Susie Hershberger

Cowboy Bars

1 C. brown sugar
1 C. oleo
1½ t. vanilla
2 C. flour
½ t. salt
1 C. coconut
¾ C. nuts

1 C. white sugar
2 eggs
¼ C. milk
1½ t. baking powder
2 C. oatmeal
1½ C. chocolate chips

Cream sugar and oleo. Add rest of ingredients. Mix well and put in a large jelly roll pan. Spread evenly and press lightly into pan. Bake at 350° for 20-30 minutes or till done.

Clara Yoder

Good Cookies

2 C. brown sugar
1 C. butter or oleo
3 eggs
2 t. soda

1 t. cream of tartar
5 T. cold water
1 t. vanilla
3½ C. flour, or more
   if needed

Cream sugar and oleo, add eggs and remaining ingredients. Drop by teaspoon on a greased cookie sheet. Bake at 350° for 12-15 minutes.

Icing

½ stick oleo
1 t. vanilla

2 T. water
powdered sugar

Brown oleo just a little to give a better flavor. Add enough powdered sugar to make icing to spreading consistency.

Mrs. Viola Miller

Cookies

4 eggs
4 C. brown sugar
2 C. oleo
2 C. sweet milk

7 C. flour
4 t. baking powder
2 t. soda

Cream sugar and oleo. Add rest of ingredients. Drop by teaspoon or roll and cut with cookie cutter. Bake at 350°.

Mrs. Jonas J.D. Miller

Angel Cookies

1/2 C. butter	2 1/2 C. flour
1/2 C. shortening	1 t. soda
1/2 C. brown sugar	1 t. cream of tartar
1/2 C. white sugar	1/2 t. salt
1 egg	1/2 C. nuts or
1 t. vanilla	chocolate chips

Cream shortenings and sugars. Add other ingredients in order given. Roll into balls the size of walnuts and dip top half in cold water then into sugar. Bake at 350° on greased cookie sheet 10-12 minutes. Yield: 3 dozen.

Mary Esta Yoder

Jello Cookies

3/4 C. oleo	3 oz. box jello (any flavor)
1/2 C. white sugar	2 1/2 C. flour
2 eggs	1 t. baking powder
1 t. vanilla	

Mix together and chill overnight. Make small balls and roll in white sugar mixed with cinnamon. Put thumbprint in center with red cinnamon candy. Bake at 375° for 10 minutes.

Mrs. Aden J. Hershberger

Hershey's Brownies

Cream together:
1 stick oleo   1 C. white sugar

Add:
4 eggs one at a time and beat well
1 can Hershey's syrup (1 1/2 C.)
1 C. Softasilk flour (measure before sifting)
1/2 C. nuts (optional)

Bake in large cookie sheet at 350° for 20 minutes.

Mrs. John J. Troyer

Chocolate Chip Cookies

2 C. Crisco
2 C. white sugar
1 C. brown sugar
8 C. flour
4 eggs

2 t. salt
2 t. soda
4 t. vanilla
2 C. chocolate chips

Blend Crisco and sugars. Add eggs and vanilla, mix well. Add combined dry ingredients and mix thoroughly. Stir in chocolate chips. Drop by teaspoon on cookie sheet. Bake at 350° until lightly browned.

Mrs. Alvin H. Schlabach

Chocolate Crispy Cookies

5 C. flour
2 t. soda
1 t. salt
2 C. oleo, softened
2 (12 oz.) pkg. chocolate chips or M&M's

4 C. sugar
4 eggs
4 t. vanilla
8 C. Rice Krispies

Beat oleo and sugar until smooth. Beat eggs and vanilla. Mix in flour, soda and salt. Stir in cereal and chips. Drop on greased baking sheet. Bake at 350° for 10 minutes or until lightly browned.

Mrs. Emanuel H. Yoder

Raisin Bars

1 C. water
  Boil 5 minutes. Cool and add:
1/2 t. soda
  Cream:
1/2 C. oleo
1 C. sugar
  Mix with raisin mixture. Sift:
2 C. flour
1 t. soda

1 C. raisins

1/2 t. salt

1 egg
1 t. vanilla

1 t. cinnamon

Add to creamed mixture. Add 1/2 C. nuts. Bake in jelly roll pan at 350°. Glaze: Blend 1 C. powdered sugar and approx. 1 T. milk. Drizzle over warm bars. When cool cut in squares.

Mrs. Paul A. Yoder

Marble Squares

2½ C. brown sugar
2½ C. white sugar
2½ C. oleo
2½ t. salt
6 eggs
3 t. vanilla

7¾ C. flour
1 t. soda
2 t. baking powder
½ t. salt
1½ C. nuts
1½ C. chocolate chips

Cream sugars, oleo, eggs and vanilla. Add flour, soda, baking powder and salt. Spread in 2 jelly roll pans. Sprinkle chips on top. Put in oven for 1 minute. Take out and marbleize with knife. Sprinkle nuts on top. Bake 20 minutes. Cool and cut in squares.

Mrs. Dan J. Bowman

Butter Cream Drops

2½ C. brown sugar (packed)
½ C. butter
½ C. soft shortening (lard)
4 eggs
4⅔ C. flour
2 t. soda

1 t. baking powder
1 t. salt
2 C. sour cream
2 t. vanilla
1 C. walnuts (optional)

Cream sugar, butter and lard thoroughly. Add eggs, mix well. Spoon flour into dry cup, level off and pour flour on wax paper. Add soda, baking powder and salt to flour. Stir to blend. Add blended dry ingredients to creamed mixture alternately with sour cream. Stir in vanilla and nuts. Drop by teaspoon onto greased cookie sheet. Bake at 350° for 10-12 minutes. Frost while warm.

Frosting

12 T. butter or oleo
3 C. powdered sugar

2 t. vanilla
8 T. hot water

Melt oleo in saucepan. Brown lightly. Remove from heat and stir in sugar and vanilla. Add water. Beat with spoon until icing reaches spreading consistency.

Mrs. David Miller

Butterscotch Tartie

6 eggs
1¼ C. white sugar
1 t. baking powder

2 C. graham cracker crumbs
1 C. chopped nuts

Beat egg yolks, add sugar and baking powder. Beat egg whites until stiff then fold in crumbs and nuts. Pour in 2" x 9" pan lined with wax paper. Bake at 325° for 30 minutes or until done. Cool. Turn pan upside down, take wax paper off and cut in small squares. Layer with sauce.

Sauce
Melt ¼ C. butter in a saucepan. Blend in 1 C. brown sugar, ¼ C. water, 1 T. flour, 1 egg, well beaten, ¼ C. orange juice or a nip of orange flavor and vanilla. Cool until thickened. Can be put in layers like date pudding with whipped cream or topping.

Mrs. Emanuel Weaver

Seven Layer Cookies

¼ lb. butter, melted in 9" x 13" pan
    Add the following in layers. Do not stir.
1 C. graham cracker crumbs (press into butter)
6 oz. pkg. chocolate chips
6 oz. pkg. butterscotch chips
1 C. coconut
1 C. nuts

Pour 1 can Eagle Brand milk over all. Bake at 325° for 25-30 minutes.

Mary Ellen Troyer

Aunt Fannie Drop Cookies

2 C. brown sugar
¾ C. sweet milk
1 t. soda
1 t. baking powder

3 eggs
1 C. lard, melted
4 C. flour
1 t. vanilla

Beat eggs, sugar, milk, lard and soda. Sift flour and baking powder. Add to first mixture. Add vanilla. Drop by teaspoon onto lightly greased baking sheet. Bake at 375°.

Mrs. Fannie Yoder

71

Date Filled Oat Cookies

2 C. shortening (half butter)
3 C. brown sugar
6 C. flour
4 C. rolled oats

1 t. salt
2 t. soda
1 C. buttermilk
1 t. vanilla

Cream sugar and shortening, add vanilla. Sift flour, add salt, soda and rolled oats. Add dry ingredients alternately with buttermilk. Mix thoroughly. Chill in refrigerator for several hours. Roll out on lightly floured board about 1/8" thick. Cut with cookie cutter and place 1" apart on greased baking sheet. Bake at 375° until golden brown. Makes 8 dozen cookies. Cool and fill with filling.

Filling

2 C. finely chopped dates
1 C. plus 2 T. water

1 C. sugar

Combine ingredients and cook until thick. Let cool before spreading between cookies.

Mrs. Adam Yoder

Chocolate Cookies

1 C. brown sugar
1 egg
1 t. vanilla
1/2 t. soda
1/2 C. cocoa

1/2 C. shortening
1/2 C. milk
1 3/4 C. sifted flour
1/2 t. salt
1/2 C. chopped nuts

Cream shortening and sugar. Add egg and remaining ingredients, adding flour and nuts last. Make balls and roll in powdered sugar, drop on cookie sheet. Bake at 350° for 8 minutes.

Mrs. Adam Yoder

Peanut Butter Squares

Cream:

¹/₂ C. white sugar	¹/₃ C. crunchy peanut
¹/₂ C. brown sugar	butter
¹/₂ C. butter or margarine, softened	1 egg, beaten

Stir together and blend into creamed mixture:

1 C. flour	¹/₂ t. baking soda
1 C. quick oats	¹/₄ t. salt

Spread in a greased 13" x 9" pan and bake at 350° for 17-22 minutes or until golden brown. Frost when cool. Yield: 4 dozen.

Frosting

Cream:
1¹/₂ C. powdered sugar
¹/₄ C. crunchy peanut butter

Stir in 2 T. milk (¹/₂ t. at a time) until spreading consistency. Reserve ¹/₃ C. of mixture. To remaining frosting, add 3 T. cocoa and 1 T. milk. Frost squares with cocoa frosting. Drop the peanut butter frosting by teaspoon onto the cocoa frosting and swirl for a marbled effect.

Mrs. Adam Yoder

Everything Cookies

1 C. margarine	1 C. salad oil
1 C. white sugar	2 T. vanilla
1 C. brown sugar	3 C. unsifted flour
1 egg, beaten	1 t. salt
1 t. cream of tartar	1 t. soda
1 C. oatmeal	1 C. Rice Krispies
1 C. coconut	1 C. chocolate chips

Mix in order given. Drop by teaspoonful on ungreased cookie sheet. Bake at 350°.

Mary Ellen Troyer

Oatmeal Cookies

2 C. brown sugar
2 eggs
1½ C. flour
1 t. soda
3 C. quick oatmeal
½ C. coconut

1 C. butter or oleo
2 t. vanilla
1 t. baking powder
¼ t. salt
1 C. chocolate chips
¼ C. walnuts

Beat together sugar, butter, eggs and vanilla. Sift together the dry ingredients and add to the above mixture. Stir in oatmeal, chocolate chips, coconut and walnuts. Refrigerate a few hours or overnight. Roll each ball in powdered sugar. Place on cookie sheet and bake at 350° for 10 minutes. They will be soft if lightly baked.

Mrs. Elmer Yoder

Cane Molasses Cookies

1 egg, beaten
1 C. shortening
1½ C. cane molasses
1 C. brown sugar
1 C. buttermilk

3 t. soda
½ t. salt
¼ t. ginger
6 C. flour

Drop and bake at 325°.

Katie Troyer

Chocolate Chip Cookies

1 C. shortening (always use
   shortening)
1½ C. flour
1 t. salt
1 t. soda
1 pkg. chocolate chips
2 C. oatmeal

1 t. vanilla
2 eggs
¾ C. brown sugar
¾ C. white sugar
1 C. nuts

Cream together sugars, shortening and vanilla until light and fluffy. Add eggs one at a time, beating well after each addition. Sift flour, salt and soda and add to sugar mixture. Fold in oatmeal, chips and nuts. Bake at 350°.

Ada Weaver

Butterscotch Oatmeal Cookies

1 C. white sugar
1 C. brown sugar
1 C. shortening
2 eggs
2 C. flour
2½ C. oatmeal

½ C. nuts
1 C. coconut
1 t. soda
1 t. baking powder
1 t. vanilla
1 C. butterscotch chips

Cream sugars and shortening. Add eggs and vanilla. Beat well. Add oatmeal and coconut. Then stir in flour, soda, baking powder, nuts and chips. Drop by teaspoon on greased cookie sheet. Bake at 375°.

Mary Ellen Troyer

Fruit Squares

3 C. flour
2 t. baking powder
2 T. sugar

1 t. salt
1 C. butter

Blend as pie crust. Add 1 C. milk and 2 egg yolks. Divide half of dough in jelly roll pan. Add pie filling. Top with rest of dough. Beat egg whites and spread on top and sprinkle with powdered sugar. Bake at 350° for 10-15 minutes.

Alma E. Stutzman

Banana Chocolate Chip Cookies

2½ C. sifted flour
2 t. baking powder
¼ t. soda
⅔ C. shortening
½ t. salt

1 C. sugar
2 eggs
1 t. vanilla
1 C. mashed ripe bananas
1 C. semisweet
    chocolate chips

Sift flour, baking powder, soda and salt. Beat shortening until creamy. Add sugar and eggs one at a time. Stir in vanilla and flour mixture alternately with bananas. Fold in chips. Drop by teaspoon on ungreased cookie sheet. Bake at 400° for 12 minutes.

Mrs. Jonas N. Borntrager

Gob Cookies

Cream together:

1 C. white sugar	2 eggs
1 C. brown sugar	1/2 C. Crisco

Add sifted dry ingredients:

4 C. all-purpose flour	1/2 t. baking powder
2 t. soda	1/2 C. cocoa
1/2 t. salt	

Add:
1 C. sour milk or 1 C. sweet milk plus 1 T. vinegar
1 t. vanilla   1 C. boiling water
Place in refrigerator while making the filling.

Filling

1 C. Crisco	1/2 t. salt
2 C. powdered sugar (or more)	1 t. vanilla

Cream above ingredients. Cook 5 T. flour and 1 C. milk to thick paste. Cool. Drop by spoonfuls into creamed mixture. Take batter, drop like cookies and bake at 400° for 7 minutes. When cookies are cooled spread with filling and put together as a sandwich. Makes 26 sandwiches. Very good!

Mrs. Jonas N. Borntrager
Mrs. Marlin Yoder

Chocolate Bars

Cream:

1/2 C. butter	2 eggs, beaten
3/4 C. white sugar	1 t. vanilla

Stir together and blend with creamed mixture:

3/4 C. flour	1/4 t. baking powder
2 T. cocoa	1/4 t. salt

Fold in 1/2 C. nuts. Spread in greased pan and bake 15-20 minutes. Spread 2 1/2 C. small marshmallows on top. Bake 2-3 minutes longer. Cool. Combine 1 C. peanut butter and 1 C. semisweet chocolate chips and stir over low heat until melted. Add 1 1/2 C. Rice Krispies. Spread on top of cooled crust and cut in bars. Keep refrigerated.

Mrs. Abe E. Mast

Butter Balls

2 C. flour, sifted
2 t. baking powder
¾ C. oleo

1 C. brown sugar
1 egg
1 t. vanilla

Cream the sugar and oleo and add the egg. Add the sifted flour and baking powder and vanilla. Chill. Roll into small balls. Roll each ball into ½ C. nuts and ½ C. white sugar. Bake at 450°.

Katie Coblentz

Thumbprint Cookies

1 C. shortening (half butter)
½ C. brown sugar
2 egg yolks
1 t. vanilla

2 C. flour
½ t. salt
2 egg whites
1 C. chopped nuts

Mix shortening, sugar, egg yolks and vanilla thoroughly. Blend in flour and salt. Take 1 teaspoon dough and roll into ball. Dip in slightly beaten egg white then roll in nuts. Place on ungreased cookie sheet 1 inch apart. Press thumb gently into center. Bake 10-12 minutes. Fill holes with frosting. Cream cheese frosting is good.

Lizzie Raber
Lizzie Ann Erb

Lemon Cookies

3 C. white sugar
1½ C. oleo
6 eggs
4 t. baking powder

4 T. lemon flavoring
7 C. Robin Hood flour
pinch of salt

Mix together. Add yellow food color to eggs. Roll and cut. Sprinkle with yellow sugar. Bake at 375° for 10 minutes.

Mrs. Henry D. Miller

Raisin Spice Drop Cookies

2 C. brown sugar
⁷/₈ C. shortening
¹/₂ C. sour milk
¹/₂ C. raisins
3 eggs, well beaten
3 C. flour

1 t. baking powder
¹/₂ t. soda
¹/₄ t. cloves
1 t. nutmeg
1 t. cinnamon

Cream sugar and shortening, add rest of ingredients. Drop by teaspoon and bake at 350°.

Mrs. Jonas N. Borntrager

Maple Leaf Cookies

1 lb. butter
4 C. brown sugar
8 eggs
6 t. soda

1 t. salt
12 T. cream
10¹/₂ C. flour
4 T. maple flavoring

Cream butter and sugar. Add remaining ingredients in order given. Do not overbake. I then use a maple leaf design cookie cutter. You may use Rich's topping for the cream.

Frosting

2 egg whites, beaten
1 T. vanilla
1 t. cream of tartar

2 T. flour
2 C. powdered sugar

Beat well. Add ¹/₂ C. Crisco and ³/₄ C. marshmallow topping. Cream till smooth.

Mrs. Dannie H. Burkholder

Orange Jello Cookies

2³/₄ C. flour
2 eggs
¹/₂ C. white sugar
3 oz. box orange jello
1 C. butter

1 t. vanilla
¹/₂ t. salt
1 t. soda
¹/₂ C. milk

Sift flour, soda and salt. Mix butter, sugar and jello. Add eggs one at a time. Add vanilla. Add flour alternately with milk. Bake on ungreased cookie sheet at 375° for 10 minutes.

Icing

2 C. powdered sugar
¹/₄ C. Crisco or butter
orange extract

¹/₄ C. milk
1 t. vanilla

Mix and spread on cookies.

Mrs. Paul A. Yoder

Sweet Milk Cookies

4 eggs
2 C. sugar
3/4 C. milk
flour as needed

1 1/2 C. shortening
2 t. soda
4 t. baking powder

Cream shortening and sugar. Add rest of ingredients. Roll out and cut with cookie cutter. Bake at 350°.

Jam Bars

2 C. rolled oats
1 3/4 C. all-purpose flour
1 C. butter or oleo
1 C. brown sugar (packed)
1/2 C. chopped nuts

1 t. cinnamon
3/4 t. salt
1/2 t. soda
3/4 C. jam preserve
(any flavor)

Combine all ingredients except jam in large bowl. Mix until mixture is crumbly. Reserve 2 C. mixture and press the rest in bottom of 9" x 13" pan. Spread jam evenly over mixture. Then sprinkle with remainder of mixture. Bake at 400° till golden brown. Cool and cut in squares.

Mrs. Eli D. Miller

Monster Cookies

1 1/2 stick oleo
1 C. white sugar
1 C. brown sugar
4 eggs
1 lb. chunky peanut butter

2 1/2 t. soda
4 C. oatmeal
1/2 lb. M&M's
12 oz. pkg. chocolate chips

Cream sugars and oleo. Add eggs one at a time then add rest of ingredients. Add more oatmeal if necessary to make a stiff dough. Form teaspoon size balls and roll in powdered sugar. Bake at 350° for 10 minutes. Do not overbake.

Mrs. Roman E. Raber
Lizzie Raber

Raisin Bars

1 C. raisins   1 C. water
   Cook together a few minutes. Cool. Add:
½ C. salad oil   1¾ C. flour
1 egg   ¼ t. salt
1 C. white sugar   1 t. soda
½ C. nuts   1 t. cinnamon

Bake in 16" x 14" pan for 15 minutes at 350°.

Mrs. Jonas J.D. Miller

Chocolate Finger Cookies

1 C. oleo   ¾ C. Hershey's cocoa
1½ C. white sugar   ¾ t. soda
3 eggs   ½ t. salt
4 C. flour   1 T. vanilla

Cream together oleo and sugar. Add remaining ingredients. Shape dough into 4" x ½" fingers. Bake at 350° for 8-10 minutes. Cool then frost with chocolate glaze. Dip in chopped nuts and garnish with a cherry half. Yields 5 dozen.

Chocolate Glaze

¼ C. oleo   1 t. vanilla
¼ C. water   6 T. Hershey's cocoa
2 C. powdered sugar

Melt oleo and add rest of ingredients and spread on cooled cookies.

Susie Hershberger

Church Cookies

2 C. brown sugar
1 C. oleo or lard
2 t. soda
4 eggs

3 t. baking powder
6 t. warm water
3-4 C. flour

Cream sugar and oleo or lard, add rest of ingredients. Drop by teaspoon onto cookie sheet and bake at 350°.

Mrs. Jonas J.D. Miller

Pumpkin Bars

4 eggs, beaten
1 C. oil
2 C. sugar
1 C. pumpkin
2 C. flour

2 t. salt
2 t. cinnamon
1 t. soda
1 t. baking powder
1 C. nuts or raisins

Bake in 17" x 11" pan at 350° for 25 minutes or until done.

Icing

3 oz. cream cheese
6 t. butter
1 t. vanilla

1¾ C. powdered sugar
1 t. milk

Soften cream cheese and butter, cream together then add remaining ingredients. Spread on bars while still warm.

Fannie Miller
Mrs. Andy J.A. Yoder
Mary Schlabach

Peanut Butter Stripe Cookies

1 C. oleo	1 t. soda
1 C. brown sugar	1/2 t. salt
1 C. white sugar	1 t. vanilla
2 eggs	2 C. flour
1 C. peanut butter	2 C. quick rolled oats

Cream oleo and sugars. Blend in remainder of ingredients. Spread dough in large greased cookie sheet.

Filling

6 oz. pkg. chocolate chips	1/4 t. salt
1/2 can Eagle Brand milk	1 t. vanilla
1 T. oleo	

Spread filling over dough and bake at 350°.

Icing

1/4 C. peanut butter	1/4 C. oleo
1 1/2 C. powdered sugar	milk

Spread on top after cookies have cooled.

Mrs. Levi H. Mast

Date Oatmeal Cookies

1 1/2 C. shortening
1 C. white sugar
2 C. brown sugar
2 eggs
1/2 C. water
2 t. vanilla
2 t. salt

3 C. flour
1 t. soda
2 t. cinnamon
1/2 t. nutmeg
4 C. quick oats
1/2 lb. dates
1 C. chopped nuts

Cut up dates and add 1 C. water. Cook over medium heat until dates are soft. Mix in bowl: shortening, sugars, eggs, water and vanilla. Add cooled dates and dry ingredients and blend well. Drop by teaspoon on greased cookie sheet. Bake at 350° for 10-15 minutes. Yields 8 dozen.

Mary Esta Yoder

Chocolate Butterscotch Bar Cookie

1/2 C. oleo
3/4 C. white sugar
2 eggs
1 t. vanilla
3/4 C. flour

1/2 C. nuts
2 T. cocoa
1/4 t. salt
1/4 t. baking powder
2 C. marshmallows

Cream oleo and sugar. Beat in eggs and vanilla. Sift flour, cocoa, baking powder and salt. Add nuts. Stir into egg mixture. Spread into bottom of 9" x 13" pan. Bake at 350° for 15-20 minutes. Sprinkle marshmallows evenly on top and bake 2 minutes. Cool. In saucepan, combine 6 oz. pkg. butterscotch or chocolate chips and 1 C. peanut butter. Melt and add 1 1/2 C. Rice Krispies. Spread mixture on top of cooled bars. Chill and cut in bars.

Katie Coblentz

Ranger Cookies

1 C. white sugar
1 C. brown sugar
1 C. shortening (scant)
2 eggs
2 C. flour (pastry)
2 C. quick oats

2 C. Rice Krispies
1 C. coconut
1 t. soda and 2 T. water
½ t. baking powder
½ t. salt
1 C. nutmeats

Cream sugars and shortening. Add beaten eggs. Beat until fluffy. Add soda in water. Add dry ingredients and drop by teaspoonful on cookie sheet. Bake at 375°. Do not overbake.

Katie Coblentz

Prizewinning Cookies

4 eggs
2 C. butter and lard
2 C. white sugar
2 C. brown sugar
2 C. sweet milk

4 t. soda
10 t. baking powder
1 t. salt
10 C. flour
4 t. vanilla

Cream butter and sugars. Add eggs and beat well. Add remaining ingredients, adding flour last. Bake at 350° until golden. Frost with brown sugar frosting or add chocolate chips.

Mrs. Mose E. Hershberger

Raisin Filled Cookies

2 C. brown sugar
1 C. sweet milk
4 t. cream of tartar
1 C. shortening
7 C. flour

2 t. soda
2 t. baking powder
2 eggs
2 t. vanilla

Cream sugar and shortening. Add remaining ingredients. Mix well. Roll out the dough and cut with cutter. Put 1 teaspoon filling on cookie, place another cookie on top which has a hole in the middle (make a hole with thimble.) Do not press together. Bake at 350° for 20 minutes or until done. Good with frosting.

Filling

2 C. chopped raisins
2 T. flour
1 C. water
  Boil till thick.

1 C. sugar
1 T. lemon juice

Mrs. Mose M. Miller

Peanut Butter Fingers

1 C. shortening
2 C. brown sugar
2/3 C. peanut butter
2 eggs
1/2 t. salt

1 t. soda
1 t. vanilla
2 C. oatmeal
2 C. flour

Cream shortening. Add sugar, peanut butter, eggs and vanilla. Add dry ingredients. Spread on large cookie sheet. Bake at 350° until nicely browned. Cool before glazing.

Glaze

3 T. water
1/2 C. cocoa
1/2 t. vanilla

2 T. butter
1 C. powdered sugar

Mix together water and butter. Bring to a boil. Remove from heat. Add cocoa, powdered sugar and vanilla. Stir until smooth then spread on bars. Cut the bars and remove from pan.

Mrs. Paul Frey

Chocolate Chip Pudding Cookies

3 1/2 C. flour
1 1/2 t. baking soda
1 1/2 C. soft butter
1 C. brown sugar
1/2 C. white sugar
3 eggs

6 oz. instant
    chocolate pudding mix
1 1/2 t. vanilla
2 C. chocolate chips
1 C. chopped nuts

Mix flour with baking soda. Cream butter and sugars, add pudding mix and vanilla in a large bowl. Beat until smooth and creamy. Beat in eggs gradually. Add flour mixture then stir in chips and nuts. Bake on ungreased cookie sheet at 375° for 8-10 minutes.

Anna Kay Bowman

Double Chocolate Bars

¹/₂ C. oleo	³/₄ C. flour
³/₄ C. white sugar	¹/₂ C. nuts
2 eggs	2 T. cocoa
1 t. vanilla	¹/₄ t. salt
¹/₄ t. baking powder	2 C. marshmallows

Cream oleo and sugar. Beat in eggs and vanilla. Add flour, cocoa, baking powder and salt. Add nuts. Spread into bottom of pan. Bake at 350° for 15-20 minutes. Sprinkle marshmallows evenly on top and bake 2 minutes. Cool. In saucepan combine 6 oz. chocolate or butterscotch chips and 1 C. peanut butter. Heat until chips are melted. Add 1¹/₂ C. Rice Krispies. Spread mixture on top of cooled bars. Chill and cut in bars.

Mrs. Henry M. Troyer
Mrs. Mose J.E. Raber
Mrs. Noah L. Yoder

Fudge Nut Bars

2 C. butter	4 C. flour
4 C. brown sugar	2 t. soda
4 eggs	2 t. salt
4 t. vanilla	6 C. quick oatmeal

Cream together butter and sugar. Add eggs and vanilla. Stir in flour, soda, salt and rolled oats.

Fudge Nut Filling

1 can Eagle Brand milk	2 T. oleo
12 oz. pkg. chocolate chips	2 t. vanilla
1 C. nuts	¹/₂ t. salt

In saucepan over low heat mix together chocolate chips, Eagle Brand milk, oleo and salt. Stir until smooth. Stir in vanilla and nuts. Spread a thin layer of oatmeal mixture in 2 cookie sheets. Then spread chocolate filling thinly over oatmeal mixture. Dot remainder of oatmeal mixture over chocolate filling. Bake at 350° for 25-30 minutes.

Mrs. Reuben Miller

Peanut Butter Fingers

1 pkg. active dry yeast	2 T. warm water
½ C. white sugar	1 egg
½ C. brown sugar	¼ C. margarine
½ C. peanut butter	¼ C. shortening
1½ C. flour	¼ t. salt
¾ t. soda	

Dissolve yeast in warm water. Mix in sugars, peanut butter, margarine and shortening until smooth. Add egg. Stir in flour, baking soda and salt. Bake in a loaf pan at 375°. Makes 6 dozen cookies.

Cocoa Glaze

1½ C. powdered sugar	¼ C. cocoa
3 T. milk	

Blend all together and drizzle over cookies.

Mrs. Jonas A. M. Yoder

Dream Bars

½ C. butter	½ C. nuts
½ C. brown sugar	½ C. coconut
1 C. flour	1 t. vanilla
2 eggs	½ t. baking powder
1 C. brown sugar	2 t. flour

Mix butter, brown sugar and flour and spread into a greased 9 inch pan. Bake at 350° for 15 minutes. Beat eggs and add brown sugar, coconut, nuts, vanilla, baking powder and flour. Spread over the baked crumbs. Bake another 15 minutes. Cut in squares.

Debbie Cookies

2 C. oleo
6 C. brown sugar
8 eggs, well beaten
2 t. salt
3 t. soda

4 t. cinnamon
1 t. nutmeg
4 t. vanilla
6 C. flour
6 C. oatmeal

Cream oleo and sugar, add eggs. Then add remaining ingredients, adding flour and oatmeal last. Bake at 325°.

Filling

2 egg whites
1 t. vanilla

3 C. powdered sugar
1 C. Crisco

Cream and spread between cookies.

Molasses Cookies

3 C. shortening
4 C. sugar
1 C. Brer Rabbit molasses
4 eggs
8 t. soda

8 C. flour
1 t. cloves
2 t. cinnamon
2 t. salt

Melt shortening, add sugar, molasses, eggs and salt. Add spices. Mix and add flour and soda. Roll into balls and roll in white sugar. Place on greased cookie sheet. Do not press down.

Edna Troyer

Chewy Oatmeal Cookies

2 C. flour
1¼ C. oleo
2 C. raisins
1½ t. soda
1 t. salt

3 C. brown sugar
4 C. quick oats
4 eggs
1 t. vanilla

Cream oleo and sugar. Add rest of ingredients. Drop by teaspoon on cookie sheet. Bake at 300°.

Filling

2 egg whites, beaten
1 t. vanilla

2 C. powdered sugar
1¼ C. Crisco

Mix and spread between cookies.

Mrs. Aden J. Raber

Molasses Cookies

2 C. white sugar
2 C. brown sugar
3½ lb. Gold Medal flour
1 C. molasses
1 C. light Karo
5 eggs

1 lb. oleo
3 T. soda
½ C. boiling water
1 C. raisins
2 C. chocolate chips
½ t. salt

Cream sugars and shortening. Add rest of ingredients. Put strips of dough on cookie sheets. Brush with beaten eggs and bake at 325°. Cut in bars before taking off cookie sheets.

Mrs. Eli A. Beachy

Chocolate Chip Bar Cookies

1 C. shortening
1¾ C. sugar
2 eggs
1 t. soda
1 t. baking powder

1 C. coffee
3½ C. flour
6 oz. pkg. chocolate chips
½ C. nuts

Cream shortening and sugar. Add rest of ingredients. Mix well and spread on a large cookie sheet. Bake at 350° for 20-25 minutes. Frost and cut into squares.

Mary Esta Yoder

Butterscotch Chocolate Bars

1½ C. oleo
2¼ C. white sugar
6 eggs
3 t. vanilla
2¼ C. flour

6 T. cocoa
¾ t. salt
1½ t. baking powder
½ C. nuts

Bake at 325° for 15-20 minutes. Top with 2 C. miniature marshmallows. Put back in oven until marshmallows are soft or a little toasted (not too hard). Take out and cool.

1 pkg. butterscotch chips (18 oz.)
2¼ C. peanut butter

4½ C. Rice Krispies

Melt chips and peanut butter in double boiler. Add Rice Krispies. Spread on top.

Mrs. Eli J. Mast

Fresh Apple Bars

3 eggs
1 C. cooking oil

1³/₄ C. white sugar

Beat above ingredients and add:

2 C. all-purpose flour
1/2 t. salt
1/2 t. cinnamon

1 t. soda
2 C. chopped fine apples
1 C. chopped nuts

Bake in large cookie sheet at 350°.

Emma Hershberger

Soft Sugar Cookies

1 lb. oleo
3 C. white sugar
4 eggs, beaten
8 C. Robin Hood flour
1/2 t. salt

2 t. soda
6 t. baking powder
2 C. cream or Pet milk
vanilla or other flavoring

Cream together oleo and sugar. Add remaining ingredients. Bake at 350° - 400°.

Mrs. Dan M. Miller

Snackin' Granola Bars

3¹/₂ C. oats
1 C. raisins
1 C. chopped nuts
2/3 C. butter or oleo, melted
1/2 C. brown sugar (packed)

1/3 C. honey, corn syrup
 or molasses
1 egg, beaten
1/2 t. vanilla
1/2 t. salt

Toast oats in ungreased large shallow pan at 350° for 15-20 minutes. Combine toasted oats with remaining ingredients. Mix well. Press firmly into well greased jelly roll pan. Bake in preheated oven at 350° for 20 minutes. Cool and cut into bars.

Mrs. Mervin Lehman

Double Cruncher Cookies

Cream together:

1/2 C. shortening	1/2 t. vanilla
1 egg	1/2 C. white sugar
1/2 C. brown sugar	

Add:

1 C. flour	1 t. salt
1/2 t. soda	1 C. coconut
1 C. rolled oats	1 C. corn flakes or
	Rice Krispies

This makes a stiff batter. Drop cookies and bake at 350°.

Filling

Melt 1 C. butterscotch chips in double boiler. Stir in 1/2 C. powdered sugar, 1 T. water and 1/2 C. cream cheese. Cream together and spread between 2 cookies.

Mrs. Henry M. Troyer

Chewy Oatmeal Cookies

1 1/2 C. brown sugar	1 t. cinnamon
3/4 C. oleo (scant)	3/4 t. soda
2 eggs	1/2 t. salt
1 1/4 C. flour	2 C. quick oats
1 t. vanilla	

Flatten with spoon dipped in water. These bake fast. Do not overbake.

Filling

1 C. powdered sugar	3/4 C. Crisco
1/2 t. vanilla	1 egg white, beaten

Cream together and spread between cookies.

Mrs. Levi Beachy

91

Cowboy Cookies

2 C. brown sugar
2 C. white sugar
  Mix together and add:
2 t. vanilla
1/2 C. milk
4 C. flour
3 t. baking powder
1/2 t. salt

2 C. oleo
4 eggs, beaten

3 C. oatmeal
1 1/2 C. coconut
2 C. chocolate chips
nuts

Mix all ingredients except nuts and spread evenly on pan. Sprinkle with nuts. Bake at 350°. Cut in squares before cooled.

Mrs. David L. Troyer

Pumpkin Cookies

2 C. brown sugar
2 eggs
1 C. lard
2 C. pumpkin

4 C. flour
2 t. baking powder
2 t. soda
2 t. cinnamon

Cream lard and sugar, add eggs and remaining ingredients, adding flour last. Add nuts, raisins or dates if desired. Bake at 350° till golden brown. Frost while still warm.

Mrs. Dan M. Miller

Vanilla Wafers

1 1/2 C. butter or oleo
3 C. white sugar
6 eggs
6 T. milk

2 t. soda
1 1/3 t. cinnamon
1 t. salt
9 C. flour

Cream butter and sugar. Add eggs and remaining ingredients. Add flour last. Bake at 350° till golden brown. For chocolate cookies add 4 t. cocoa.

Frosting

8 T. butter or oleo
3-4 T. cream

vanilla
powdered sugar

Add enough powdered sugar to desired thickness. Spread between 2 cookies.

Mrs. Henry M. Troyer

Patties

2 eggs
1 t. sugar
¼ t. salt

1 C. milk
1 C. flour (or more)

Stir eggs well with fork and add sugar. Add flour and milk alternately. A smooth batter is important.

Mrs. Nelson A. Barkman

Graham Crackers

1 C. brown sugar
1 C. butter or lard
1 C. maple syrup
½ C. sour milk or buttermilk
1 C. baking molasses

1 egg
½ t. salt
2 t. soda
1 t. vanilla
graham flour to make stiff

Cream butter and sugar. Add remaining ingredients. Roll out and bake at 350°.

Mrs. Henry E. Mast

Snowballs

½ C. butter or oleo
2 T. sugar
1 t. vanilla

1 C. all-purpose flour
1 C. chopped nuts
powdered sugar

Mix butter, sugar and vanilla. Gradually stir in flour and nuts. Chill. Shape in marble size balls. Bake on ungreased cookie sheet at 350° for 15-17 minutes or until firm but not brown. Roll in powdered sugar, cool and sugar again. Makes about 50 snowballs.

Mrs. Roy A. Schlabach

- Notes -

Desserts

Apple Pudding

2 C. brown sugar
2 eggs
½ C. vegetable oil
1 t. vanilla
2 t. soda

2 C. flour
2 C. diced cooked apples
1 t. cinnamon
½ C. nuts
½ t. salt

Bake at 350° for 55 minutes or till done like a cake.

Sauce

3 C. water
1½ C. brown sugar

pinch of salt

Cook then add 4 T. clear jel mixed with water and add to mixture. Bring to boil again. Cool. Can be mixed with whipped cream. Fix in pan or in layers.

Mrs. David D. Miller

Rhubarb Crunch

Mix until crumbly:
1 C. flour
¾ C. oatmeal
1 C. brown sugar (packed)

½ C. melted butter
1 t. cinnamon

Cover with 4 C. diced rhubarb. Combine the following:

1 C. sugar
1 C. water

2 T. cornstarch
1 t. vanilla

Press half of crumbs in a greased 9" baking pan. Add diced rhubarb. Combine second mixture and cook until thick and clear. Pour over rhubarb. Top with remaining crumbs. Bake at 350° for 1 hour.

Mrs. John A. Weaver

Pinescotch Pudding

2 eggs, beaten
1 C. sugar
   Fold in:
1 C. crushed pineapple
1 C. nuts
   Add and sift together:
$^3/_4$ C. flour
1 t. baking powder
$^1/_4$ t. salt

Bake and cut in squares when cold.

Sauce

$^1/_4$ C. butter   1 C. brown sugar
$^1/_4$ C. pineapple juice   1 egg
$^1/_4$ C. water

Cook this together a few minutes. Cool and add whipped cream. Pour over cake squares. Put whipped cream on top if desired.

Mrs. Eli D. Miller

Layered Pudding

1$^1/_4$ C. Bisquick   3 T. oleo
1 T. brown sugar (packed) $^1/_4$ C. chocolate chips

Bake in 350° oven. Cream together Rich's topping and softened cream cheese, then mix 1 box chocolate instant pudding with 1$^1/_2$ C. milk and put on top of whip mixture. Mix 1 box vanilla instant pudding with 1$^1/_2$ C. milk and put on top of chocolate pudding. Top with Rich's topping and nuts.

Mrs. Emanuel Weaver

Butterscotch Chip Pudding

Put $^1/_2$ C. milk in double boiler with 1 bag marshmallows. Heat till melted. Put chips in when cooled. When cold add 1 C. whipped cream. Put in layers with graham crackers.

Mrs. Atlee J. Miller

97

Graham Cracker Fluff

2 egg yolks
1/2 C. sugar
2/3 C milk
1 pkg. gelatine
1/2 C. cold water
2 egg whites

1 C. whipping cream
1 t. vanilla
3 T. melted butter
3 T. sugar
12 graham crackers

Beat egg yolks and add sugar and milk. Cook until slightly thickened. Soak gelatine in cold water. Pour hot mixture over softened gelatine and stir till smooth. Chill till slightly thickened. Add stiffly beaten egg whites, vanilla and whipped cream to chilled mixture. Combine melted butter, cracker crumbs and sugar to make crumb mixture. Sprinkle half of crumbs in bottom of dish then put in pudding mixture and put rest of crumbs on top. Let chill till set.

Mrs. Mary E. Mast

Graham Cracker Fluff

Soak 1 pkg. gelatine in 1/3 C. cold water
1/2 C. sugar
2/3 C. rich milk
2 egg yolks

Mix together. Cook in double boiler until it boils only 1 minute. Remove from heat and add gelatine and 1 t. vanilla. Set in cool place until it begins to thicken then add stiffly beaten egg whites and 1 C. cream which has been whipped. Mix 3 T. brown sugar, 3 T. butter and 12 graham crackers crushed for crumb mixture. Put in layers or as preferred.

Mrs. Roy J. Wengerd

Frozen Dessert

1 box vanilla wafers
1 stick butter
2 C. powdered sugar
2 squares melted chocolate
　　or 2 oz. chocolate chips
2 egg yolks, well beaten
2 egg whites, well beaten
1/2 C. nuts
1 t. vanilla
1/2 gal. vanilla ice cream

Crush cookies and spread in bottom of pan, saving some for top. Cream the butter and powdered sugar. Add egg yolks, melted chocolate and nuts. Beat until fluffy. Stir in beaten egg whites and vanilla. Spread over the crumbs. Put ice cream evenly over this. Sprinkle some cookie crumbs over the top. Place in freezer until ready to serve. Have the ice cream soft.

Mrs. Mose A. Miller

Chocolate Éclair Dessert

1 box graham crackers
9 oz. Cool Whip
2 C. vanilla instant
　　pudding mix
5 C. milk

Prepare pudding: Heat milk to almost boiling. Cool, then add pudding mix. Fold in Cool Whip. Line bottom of 9" x 13" pan with whole graham crackers. Put half of pudding mixture over crackers. Make another layer of crackers. Add remaining pudding. Top with another layer of crackers.

Topping

1 C. chocolate chips
3 T. margarine
3 T. milk
2 T. corn syrup
1 T. vanilla
1 1/2 C. powdered sugar

Melt chocolate chips and margarine. Add remaining ingredients. Stir well and spread over crackers. Refrigerate at least 1 day before serving.

Mrs. Noah L. Yoder
Mrs. Dan C. Yoder
Fannie Troyer

Fresh Fruit Dish

Take 2 C. juice of pineapple or orange and thicken just a little with clear jel (like a very thin gravy). You can let this set a few days. Sweeten just a little. Can also use honey. When ready to use cut up 6-8 good eating apples (Red or Yellow Delicious), 1 can pineapple chunks, 3-4 oranges, fresh grapes (1-2 C.) and bananas. When ready to use put juice over cut up fruit and serve. You may substitute fruit or not use all of the above. Honey is also good over fruit.

Mrs. Daniel E. Schlabach

Danish Fruit Dessert

3 C. water
$^2/_3$ C. sugar
$^1/_2$ C. jello (any flavor)

2 T. clear jel
pinch of salt

Heat 2 C. water to boiling. Make a paste with dry ingredients and rest of water. Stir in boiling water. If too thick when cold, add water. If fresh fruit is mixed in same as jello flavor, this makes good pie filling.

Mrs. John A. Weaver

Baked Chocolate Fudge Pudding

Cream together:
3 T. oleo
   Add:
1 C. flour
$1^1/_2$ t. baking powder
$^1/_2$ t. salt

$^3/_4$ C. white sugar

$^1/_2$ C. milk
$^1/_2$ C. nuts

Put in ungreased pan. Mix 1 C. brown sugar, $^1/_4$ C. cocoa and $^1/_4$ t. salt and sprinkle over top of batter. Do not stir. Pour $1^1/_4$ C. hot water over top of batter. Bake at 350°. Serve warm with ice cream or cold with whipped topping.

Mrs. J.L. Miller

Pie Filling Crunch Dessert

1½ C. flour
¾ C. rolled oats
1 C. brown sugar

½ t. soda
½ t. salt
½ C. softened oleo

Mix like pie dough crumbs. Put half of crumbs in 9" x 9" pan. Then add your favorite pie filling and the rest of the crumbs. Delicious when served warm with milk.

Graham Cracker Pudding

Bring 6 C. milk to a boil. Make a paste with 6 T. cornstarch, 3 egg yolks, some milk and 1½ C. white sugar. Stir in hot milk. Cook till thick and add 3 t. vanilla or maple flavoring. Prepare 2 pkg. Dream Whip and blend into thickening. Arrange with graham crackers and bananas.

Edna Troyer

Pretzel Pudding

2½ C. pretzels crushed (not fine)
1 C. brown sugar
½ C. melted butter

Mix the above and line in a 9" x 13" pan. Save some for top.

Cream Filling
8 oz. pkg. cream cheese
1 C. white sugar
2 t. vanilla

Mix:

2 boxes orange jello
2 C. whipped topping, beaten stiff

½ C. boiling water

Dissolve jello in boiling water. Mix whipped topping with jello and cream filling. Pour in pan. Sprinkle rest of crust on top.

Mrs. Elmer Yoder

Angel Food Dessert

Break up 1 angel food cake in bite size pieces in a large oblong pan. Mix 2 boxes instant vanilla pudding as directed and pour over cake. Spread your favorite pie filling on top of that (fresh strawberry or peach is delicious). Whip 2 C. Rich's topping and add 8 oz. cream cheese, softened, and ½ C. powdered sugar. Spread on top. Sprinkle graham cracker crumbs over top and chill several hours before serving.

Hint: When preparing instant pudding always heat unpasteurized milk and cool completely to prevent the soapy taste.

Mary Esta Yoder

Apple Dessert

1 C. pineapple juice plus water
1 C. crushed pineapples
1 box strawberry jello
2 large apples, chopped

½ C. nuts
1½ C. whipped cream
¾ C. sugar

Drain pineapple and heat juice. Dissolve jello in juice. Cool until partly set. Fold in pineapple, apples, nuts and whipped cream to which sugar has been added. Chill until set.

Mrs. David D. Miller

Cheesecake

2 (3 oz.) pkg. orange jello
2 C. hot water
1 C. white sugar

2 (8 oz.) pkg. cream cheese
1 t. vanilla
1 can Carnation milk

Pour hot water over jello. Set aside to cool. Beat cream cheese, sugar and vanilla. Whip Carnation milk. Pour jello and milk into cream cheese. Press graham cracker crumbs in bottom of pan. Pour mixture on crumbs.

Mrs. Paul E. Miller

Orange Danish Dessert

Bring to boil:
4 C. water
1/2 C. clear jel

1 1/4 C. white sugar
1 pkg. orange or cherry
Kool-Aid

Cool. Add fresh or canned fruit.

Mrs. Wyman D. Miller

Pink Apple Dessert

1 C. crushed pineapple
1 C. pineapple juice plus water
1 pkg. strawberry jello

2 large apples, cut up
1/3 C. chopped walnuts
1 1/2 C. whipped cream

Drain crushed pineapple. Heat juice and water to boiling. Dissolve jello in this and cool until partly set. Fold in apples, pineapple and walnuts. Fold in whipped cream. We add cottage cheese yet. Pour into dish or mold. Chill until set.

Mrs. Jonas J. Miller

Caramel Pudding

1/2 C. milk
1/2 C. white sugar

1 T. butter
2 t. baking powder

Add enough flour to make a medium dough. Drop in sauce made of:

1 1/2 C. brown sugar
1/2 C. boiling water
1 T. butter

1 t. vanilla
pinch of salt

Bake, cool and serve with whipped cream.

Jimmy Carter Pudding

1st Layer:
1 C. flour
1 stick oleo

²/₃ C. salted chopped
peanuts

Mix and press into 9" x 13" pan. Bake at 350° for 20 minutes. Cool.

2nd Layer:
¹/₃ C. peanut butter
1 C. powdered sugar

8 oz. cream cheese
1 C. whipped cream

Mix and spread over baked crust.

3rd Layer:
3 oz. box instant chocolate pudding
3 oz. box instant vanilla pudding
2³/₄ C. milk

4th Layer:
Whipped cream to cover top of pudding. Sprinkle with chopped peanuts.

Mrs. William Kuhns

Pineapple Cool Whip Salad

In large bowl mix:
1 C. white sugar

16 oz. can crushed pineapple

In saucepan:
6 T. cold water

2 pkg. Knox gelatine

Bring to boil. Pour over sugar and pineapples and stir. Put in refrigerator and let set slightly.

2 large carrots, shredded
1 C. cottage cheese
1 C. chopped nuts

1 C. chopped celery
16 oz. Cool Whip
1¹/₂ C. mayonnaise

Mix with mixture in bowl and let set for 2 hours.

Mrs. Dannie H. Burkholder

104

Upside-Down Date Pudding

1 C. pitted dates, cut up
1 C. boiling water
1 1/2 C. sifted flour
1/2 t. baking powder
1 C. chopped walnuts
1/2 C. white sugar

1 t. soda
1/2 C. brown sugar
1/2 t. salt
1 egg
2 T. butter

Combine dates and water. Blend sugars, egg and butter. Stir together dry ingredients. Add to sugar mixture. Stir in nuts and cooled date mixture. Pour into 11" x 7" baking dish. Top with:

Brown Sugar Sauce

1 1/2 C. brown sugar
1 T. butter

1 1/2 C. boiling water

Bake at 375° for 40 minutes. Cut in squares. Invert on plates. Serve warm with whipped cream.

Mrs. Clara Mast

Crow Nest Pudding

1 C. sugar
1/2 C. milk
butter (size of a walnut)

1 egg
1 t. vanilla
1 t. baking powder
(heaping)

Mix in some flour. Make slightly stiffer than cake batter. Bake. When cool cut into squares and layer.

Filling

brown butter (size of a walnut)
1 pint milk and water
2 T. flour

1/2 C sugar
2 T. vanilla

Mix together, boil. Pour over cake squares while filling is still warm. Serve.

Mrs. John A. Weaver

Orange Danish Dessert

1 qt. water   1 1/4 C. sugar

Bring to a boil and thicken with 1/2 C. clear jel. Last, stir in 1 pkg. orange Kool-Aid. Add pineapple, grapes, bananas or whatever you wish. Very tasty for children's lunch buckets.

Mrs. Dannie H. Burkholder

Date Pudding

1 C. dates (cut fine)   1 C. hot water
1 t. soda

Pour hot water over dates and soda. Cool. Add:

1 C. brown sugar   1 egg
1 T. butter   1 C. nuts
1 C. flour

Mix all together and bake at 350°.

Katie N. Miller

Butterscotch Tapioca

6 C. boiling water   1 1/2 C. pearl tapioca
1 t. salt

Cook 15 minutes. Add 2 C. brown sugar. Cook till done, stirring often. Mix together:

2 eggs, beaten   1 C. milk
1/2 C. white sugar

Add this to tapioca mixture. Cook until it bubbles. Brown 1 stick butter and add 1 t. vanilla. Cool and add whipped cream, bananas and diced Milky Way candy bar if desired.

Mrs. Albert A. Raber, Jr.

Fudge Sundae Pie

1/4 C. corn syrup	3 T. oleo
2 T. brown sugar	2 1/2 C. Rice Krispies

Combine syrup, sugar and oleo and cook over low heat until mixture begins to boil. Remove from heat and add Rice Krispies. Press evenly in pie pan. Mix:

1/4 C. peanut butter	3 T. light Karo
1/4 C. fudge sauce	

Spread half of mixture over crust. Spread 1 quart vanilla ice cream over mixture. Freeze. Before serving, warm remaining sauce and drizzle over the top.

Mrs. Delbert R. Troyer

Fudge Sundae Pie

Crust:

1/4 C. corn syrup	3 T. margarine or butter
2 T. packed brown sugar	2 1/2 C. Rice Krispies

Hot Chocolate Sauce for pie:

1 C. white sugar	1 C. water
3 T. cocoa	3 1/2 T. flour (level)
1/2 t. salt	1 t. vanilla

Cook 3 minutes. Add vanilla. Add a little peanut butter and 3 T. Karo. Put some sauce on crust, then add ice cream and top with remaining sauce. Freeze.

Mrs. Adam Yoder

Hot Fudge Sundae Cake

1 C. flour
3/4 C. sugar
2 T. cocoa
2 t. baking powder
1/4 t. salt

1/2 C. milk
2 T. salad oil
1 t. vanilla
1 C. nuts

Combine first five ingredients in an ungreased 9" x 9" pan. Mix in milk, oil and vanilla until smooth. Add nuts. Spread evenly in pan. Sprinkle with 1 C. brown sugar, then 1/4 C. cocoa. Do not mix. Pour 1 3/4 C. hot water on top of this. Bake at 350° for 40 minutes. Let stand 15 minutes. Invert each helping on plate. Top with ice cream and sauce.

Hot Fudge Sauce

3 T. oleo
1 C. sifted powdered sugar
1 t. vanilla

3 T. cocoa
1 C. evaporated milk

Melt oleo in saucepan over medium heat. Add powdered sugar and cocoa alternately with the milk. Beat until smooth. Bring to a boil on medium heat, stirring constantly. Cook 2 minutes. Add vanilla. Serve hot over ice cream.

Erma Yoder

Montana Tapioca

5 C. milk
10 T. minute tapioca

Simmer 15 minutes. Do not boil. Stir often. Add:

2 eggs, beaten
1 1/3 C. white sugar
1 t. salt
1 t. vanilla

Mix with milk and tapioca. Bring to a boil. Cool in water. When cold add beaten Rich's topping or softened cream cheese if you wish to make it more fluffy.

Mrs. Atlee J. Miller

Angel Food Pudding

6 oz. pkg. chocolate chips
6 T. water
6 T. white sugar

4 egg whites, beaten
4 egg yolks, beaten
2 C. whipped topping

Melt chocolate chips in double boiler. Add water and sugar. Then add 4 egg yolks, beaten. Bring to boil. When cool add beaten egg whites and 2 C. whipped topping. Cut angel food cake in pieces and put in layers in dish.

Mrs. Nelson A. Barkman

Cinnamon Pudding

Step 1:
2 C. brown sugar
2 T. butter

1½ C. cold water

Bring to a boil. Then add:

Step 2:
1 C. white sugar
1 C. milk
2 t. baking powder

2 T. butter
2 t. cinnamon
flour to make batter

Mix in order given. Best if dough is not too stiff.

Ada J. Yoder

Pudding

First layer:
1 C. flour
½ C. oleo

½ C. nuts

Make crumbs and press in pan and bake at 350° for 10 minutes.

1 C. powdered sugar
8 oz. cream cheese

1 C. whipped topping or
    Cool Whip

Mix and put on top of crust.

1 box instant vanilla pudding
1 box instant butterscotch pudding

3 C. milk

Mix and put on top of cream cheese layer. Then top with remainder of Cool Whip or whipped topping.

Mrs. Adam Yoder

Fruit Pizza

½ C. butter
¾ C. sugar
1 egg

1½ C. flour
1 t. baking powder
¼ t. salt

Cream butter, sugar and egg. Add remainder of ingredients and bake at 350° for 10 minutes or until lightly brown.

8 oz. cream cheese
½ C. white sugar

½ t. vanilla

Spread crushed pineapple over top. Top with fresh fruit of your choice. Garnish with ¼ C. orange marmalade and 1 T. water.

Lizzie Raber
Verna Miller

Fruit Pizza

Crust:
½ C. melted butter
1 egg

¾ C. sugar

Cream and add:
1 t. cream of tartar
½ t. soda

¼ t. salt
1⅜ C. flour

Bake at 350° for 8-10 minutes. Let cool.

8 oz. cream cheese
2 t. pineapple juice

½ C. sugar

Mix and spread over cooled crust. Put fresh fruit on next. Use at least 3 different kinds.

Glaze: Mix fruit juice with 4 T. cornstarch. Cook till thick. Let cool. Pour over fruit.

Mrs. Nelson A. Barkman

Ritz Cracker Ice Cream Dessert

50 Ritz crackers, crushed
1/4 C. oleo
1/2 C. nuts

Mix together and press in a 9" x 13" pan. Keep out 3/4 C. crumbs for on top.

6 C. ice cream
2 pkg. instant pudding (any flavor)
1 C. milk

Mix milk and ice cream together. Add pudding mix. Beat all together and pour over crumb crust. Put remaining crumbs on top.

Mrs. Viola Miller

Treasure Chest Ice Cream Pie

2 C. Rice Krispies, slightly crushed
1/2 C. brown sugar
1/3 C. melted butter or oleo
1/2 C. chopped nuts
1/2 C. coconut
1 qt. vanilla ice cream, softened

Mix together Rice Krispies, nuts and coconut and brown in the oven. Stir in sugar and butter. Put half in 9" x 9" pan. Spoon in the ice cream and put other half of crumbs on top. Freeze. You can also line pie pans with crust and make like a pie.

Ada Mae Raber

Oreo Pudding

1st Layer:
Crush Oreo cookies to form crust.

2nd Layer:
8 oz. cream cheese   1½ C. whipped topping
1 C. powdered sugar
   Mix and add to first layer.

3rd Layer:
1 box instant chocolate pudding. Mix as directed.

4th Layer:
Whipped topping. Sprinkle with crushed Oreo cookies. Serve.

Mrs. Adam Yoder
Mrs. Roman Raber

Oreo Pudding Dessert

1 lb. pkg. Oreo cookies

Crush cookies to form crumbs and reserve ¼ C. crumbs. Mix cookie crumbs and ½ C. melted margarine and press into a 13 x 9 inch pan.

2 (3 oz.) boxes vanilla instant pudding
8 oz. cream cheese
3½ C. milk

Mix together and spread on crust. Top with 4 oz. Cool Whip or whipped topping. Put reserved crumbs on top.

Mrs. Roy A. Miller
Ada J. Yoder

112

Ritz Cracker Dessert

60 Ritz crackers
1 stick melted butter
2 boxes instant butter
  pecan pudding

2 C. milk
1 qt. vanilla ice cream
8 oz. Cool Whip
3 Heath bars

Crush Ritz crackers and mix with butter. Then mix pudding, milk and ice cream together. Put pudding mixture on top of crackers. Chill 20 minutes. Put Cool Whip on top of pudding mixture, chip Heath bars on top. Keep frozen till ready to serve. Delicious.

Mrs. Aden D. Troyer

Fruit Pizza

$^1/_2$ C. butter
$^1/_2$ C. brown sugar
1 egg

1$^1/_3$ C. flour
1 t. baking powder
pinch of salt

Cream together butter, sugar and egg. Add flour, baking powder and salt. Press in a greased pizza pan. Bake at 375° for 10 minutes or till light brown.

8 oz. cream cheese
$^1/_2$ C. powdered sugar

$^1/_2$ t. vanilla
1 T. milk

Cream together and spread over crust. Arrange in a circle: fresh or canned fruit such as apples, peaches, pineapple, cherries, strawberries, oranges or bananas.

Glaze

2 C. pineapple juice or other fruit
  juice (add water if not enough)
$^1/_2$ C. sugar

1 T. clear jel (heaping)
1-2 T. jello (lemon, orange
  or strawberry)

Cook till clear. Cool. Dribble over fruit.

Mrs. Aden J. Raber

Chocolate Cookie Pudding

1 pkg. Oreo cookies (crush cookies and put in bottom of pan)

2nd Layer:
8 oz. cream cheese   1 C. whipped topping
1 C. powdered sugar

3rd Layer:
1 box vanilla instant pudding
1 box chocolate instant pudding
3 C. milk

Mix and put on top of second layer. Top with whipped topping and cookie crumbs.

Mrs. John A. Miller

Slush

2 C. white sugar   18 oz. 7-Up
3 C. boiling water   fresh peaches, cut up
12 oz. frozen orange juice   6-8 bananas, cut up

Place in freezer. Stir until partly frozen or fruit stays on top. Freeze. You may add any fruit you wish.

Mrs. Roman E. Raber

Peach Slush

1 peck peaches, sliced
2 (20 oz.) cans pineapple, crushed
1 can frozen orange juice concentrate
8 bananas

Cook 4 C. sugar and 4 C. water. Add to fruit mixture and put in boxes and freeze.

Mrs. Dan J. Bowman

Slush

2 C. white sugar
3 C. water
   Boil together and cool. Add:
6 oz. frozen orange juice
6 bananas, sliced
20 oz. can crushed pineapples

Freeze. Serve partly thawed.

Mrs. Mose E. Hershberger

Fruit Slush

1 can Tree Sweet orange juice
1½ C. white sugar
2½ cans warm water (scant)
2 cans cold water
20 oz. can crushed pineapple
8 bananas

Freeze. Thaw about 1 hour before serving.

Mrs. John J. Troyer

Orange Slush

   Boil:
2 C. white sugar   3 C. water
   Cool and add:
6 oz. frozen orange juice   20 oz. can crushed
6 bananas   pineapple

Mix together and freeze.

Mrs. John A. Miller

Orange Slush

3 C. hot water
2 C white sugar
1 C. crushed pineapples

6 oz. frozen orange juice
6 bananas

Dissolve sugar in hot water. Add orange juice. Combine pineapples and bananas. Mix together and freeze. A refreshing dessert.

Mrs. Henry D. Miller

Sherbet

2 C. water
1 C. sugar
  Boil together and add:
1 C. jello (any flavor)

Chill till partly set and add 2 quarts milk and freeze in ice cream freezer.

Mrs. Eli D. Miller

Dairy Queen Ice Cream

Soak:
2 envelopes Knox gelatine in ½ C. cold water.

Heat:
4 C. whole milk until hot but not boiling. Remove from heat.

Add:
Gelatine, 2 C. sugar, 2 t. vanilla, 1 t. salt. Cool and add 3 C. cream. Put in refrigerator and chill 5-6 hours before freezing. Makes 1 gallon.

Mrs. Henry E. Schlabach

Homemade Ice Cream

4 (3 oz.) boxes instant vanilla pudding
12 eggs
1 box freezing mix
2 C. brown sugar
1 C. white sugar

3 cans Pet milk
1 t. vanilla
1 t. maple flavoring
2 cans Eagle Brand milk

Add enough milk to fill the can and freeze. Makes an 8 quart freezer. Makes delicious ice cream.

Mrs. Aden J. Hershberger

Homemade Ice Cream

4 eggs
2 C. brown sugar
2 (3 oz.) boxes instant vanilla pudding

1 pt. cream
pinch of salt
vanilla

Milk to fill a 6 quart freezer ³/₄ full.

Mrs. Merlin Troyer

Ice Cream

6 eggs, separated
¹/₂ C. flour
¹/₂ C. cornstarch
milk

3 C. sugar
¹/₂ t. salt
vanilla

Bring 3 quarts milk to a boil. Combine flour, cornstarch, egg yolks, salt and ¹/₂ C. sugar. Add cold milk to make a thin paste. Pour the boiling milk in the mixture, stirring while you pour. This should get thick and smooth. Add 2 C. sugar. Beat the egg whites and add alternately to mixture with ¹/₂ C. sugar. Also add 1 pint of cream. Freeze. Makes 1¹/₂ gallon.

For peanut butter ice cream add ³/₄ C. peanut butter (or amount to suit your taste) to the mixture as soon as you pour in the boiling milk.

Mrs. Joe H. Bowman

Ice Cream Sandwiches

3 C. milk
1 1/2 T. gelatine
3/4 C. brown sugar

1/4 t. salt
2 C. whipped cream
3 t. vanilla

Scald milk. Add sugar and salt till dissolved. Soak gelatine in cold water. Add gelatine to milk. Mix. Cool and add vanilla. Pour in freezing tray. Freeze till firm throughout. Remove from tray. Put in a bowl and break into small pieces with a spoon. Whip and beat together the cream and frozen mixture till free from hard lumps. Return to freezing tray.

Cookie Part

2 C. brown sugar
1 C. lard
2 eggs
1 t. vanilla
1 C. sour cream
pinch of salt

2 t. soda
4-5 C. flour
6 T. cocoa
1 t. cinnamon
1/2 t. ginger

Cream together sugar and lard, add rest of ingredients. Bake cookies at 350°. Cool, put ice cream between cookies and freeze.

Mrs. Henry M. Troyer

Ice Cream Pudding

2 C. flour
1 C. nuts

1/2 C. butter or enough
to make crumbly

Mix and put in bottom of pan and bake at 350° until light brown. Cool. Reserve some of crumbs for on top.

1/2 gallon vanilla ice cream
1 box instant vanilla pudding
2 boxes instant butter pecan pudding
1 C. milk
2 C. whipped topping

Mix milk and instant puddings. Add topping and softened ice cream. Pour over crust and refrigerate.

Mrs. J.L. Miller

118

Ice Cream Pudding

2 rolls snack crackers, crushed
1/2 C. margarine, melted
1/2-1 C. chopped nuts

Mix together and press 2/3 of mixture into 13" x 9" pan.

1 box instant vanilla pudding
1 box instant butterscotch pudding
1 1/2 C. milk
1 qt. vanilla ice cream, softened
8 oz. whipped topping

Mix puddings and milk until thickened. Add remainder of ingredients and pour over crust. Sprinkle remaining crumbs on top.

Mrs. Adam Yoder

Ice Cream Pudding

50 Ritz crackers
1 stick butter
2 boxes instant pudding

1 1/2 C. milk
1 1/2 qt. soft ice cream

Crush crackers, add melted butter and put in pan. Save some for top. Mix pudding and milk. Beat 2 minutes and add ice cream. Put on top of crumbs. Sprinkle with remaining crumbs. This is a small batch.

Mrs. Merlin Troyer

Ice Cream Cake

1 chocolate cake, cut in squares
ice cream
hot fudge sauce

Put ice cream on cake and top with hot fudge and whipped cream with maraschino cherries on top.

Mrs. Merlin Troyer

Fudgesicles

1 box instant chocolate pudding
1/2 C. white sugar
3 eggs
4 C. milk

Beat together and freeze.

Mrs. Adam Yoder

Danish Pastry

2 1/2 C. flour
pinch of salt
1 C. Crisco

1 egg yolk
2/3 C. milk

Makes one cookie sheet. Beat egg white and put on top of crust. Dough is a little hard to handle so roll loosely on rolling pin and unroll into pan.

Fruit

1 qt. fruit
7 T. clear jel

3 C. sugar (scant)
1 box jello (same flavor
    as fruit)

Add enough water to right consistency. I use 1 qt. fruit per cookie sheet. It makes 20 pieces.

Maple Sponge

2 boxes vanilla pudding, cooked
3 pkg. Knox gelatine
1 C. brown sugar
4 C. boiling water
1 1/2 t. maple flavoring

Let this jel. When hard, chop it up and put in pudding. Add some whipped cream and peanuts.

Mrs. Henry E. Mast

Ice Cream

1 box instant vanilla pudding
1 box instant butter pecan pudding or any other flavor
4 eggs
½ C. white sugar
½ C. brown sugar
1 pt. cream, whipped
vanilla
enough milk to fill can ¾ full

Separate eggs. Whip whites of eggs and add white sugar. Whip again. Whip egg yolks and add brown sugar. Add instant puddings and milk. Beat well and add egg whites to mixture. Add whipped cream last. This makes 1 gallon.

Mrs. J.L. Miller

Yogurt

Heat 1½ qt. milk to 180°. Let cool to 130°. Add 3 T. plain Dannon yogurt, mixed with a little milk. Mix 1 T. gelatine in ¼ C. cold water and let set 5 minutes. When milk is reduced to 130° add the gelatine and 2 t. vanilla. Let set overnight before serving.

*"The reason people blame things
on previous generations is that there's
only one other choice."*

- Notes -

Pies

Peanut Butter Pie

8 oz. cream cheese, stir until creamy
8 oz. Eagle Brand milk
3/4 C. peanut butter
3 T. ReaLemon
1 t. vanilla
1 C. whipped topping

Mix together and put in baked pie shell.

Ada Burkholder

Eggnog Pie

1 t. gelatine
1 T. cold water
1 C. milk
1/2 C. white sugar
2 T. cornstarch

1/2 t. salt
3 egg yolks, beaten
1 T. butter
1 T. vanilla
1 C. whipping cream

Soak gelatine in cold water. Scald milk. Combine sugar, cornstarch and salt and mix well. Add to milk and cook until thick. Add eggs and cook a little longer. Add butter and gelatine. Cool then fold in whipped cream and pour in baked pie shell.

Mrs. Henry U. Burkholder

Coconut Macaroon Pie

1 1/2 C. sugar
2 eggs
1/2 t. salt
1/2 C. soft butter

1 T. flour
3/4 C. milk
1 1/2 C. coconut

Beat sugar, salt and eggs. Add butter and flour. Blend well and add milk. Fold in 1 C. coconut. Pour in unbaked pie shell. Put 1/2 C. coconut on top. Bake at 300°.

Mrs. Henry E. Mast

Apple Pie

Cook:
1 T. clear jel heaping   1 C. brown sugar
1 C. water
Add:
3/4 t. cinnamon   pinch of salt
butter
Stir in:
3/4 qt. fine apples

This makes 1 pie. To can, cold pack 1/2 hour.

Crumbs

1 C. flour   1/2 t. soda
1/4 C. brown sugar   1/2 t. cream of tartar
1/4 C. butter

Bake in unbaked crust. This makes enough for 1 pie.

Mrs. Abe E. Mast

Sour Cream Apple Pie

2 eggs, beaten   1 t. vanilla
3/4 C. white sugar   1 t. apple pie spice
1 C. sour cream   pinch of salt
2 T. flour   2 C. sliced apples

Topping

1/3 C. brown sugar   1 t. apple pie spice
1/3 C. flour   1/4 C. butter

Mix till crumbly. Bake at 350° for 30-40 minutes. Also delicious with sliced fresh peaches instead of apples.

Mrs. J.L. Miller

Union Pie

1 C. sour cream
1 C. sour milk
1 C. white sugar
1 C. maple flavored Karo
2 eggs, beaten

3 T. flour
1/2 t. soda
1 t. cinnamon
1 t. nutmeg

Mix together. Bake in 2 unbaked crusts.

Mrs. Ben E. Yoder

Mince Pie

3 C. bread crumbs
3 C. white sugar
1/2 C. butter
1/2 C. vinegar
1 C. raisins

1 t. cloves
1 t. allspice
1 t. nutmeg
3 C. water

Mix all together. Makes 4 pies.

Mrs. Ben E. Yoder

Sour Cherry Pie

1 qt. sour cherries
1 qt. water
2 C. white sugar

1/2 t. cherry flavor
pinch of salt
red food color

Thicken with:
4 T. clear jel (heaping)

1/4 C. white sugar

Moisten with water. Heat the first ingredients to boiling then add the last two. Makes 3 pies.

Mrs. Emanuel H. Yoder

Butterscotch Pie

2 C. brown sugar
3½ C. boiling water
½ t. salt

1 t. vanilla
½ C. butter

Boil these ingredients and set aside.

3 eggs
1 C. white sugar
1⅓ C. flour

3 C. milk
pinch of salt

Mix and add to brown sauce and cook until thick. Pour into 3 baked pie shells.

Mary Ann Yoder

Butterscotch Pie

2 egg yolks
1 C. brown sugar
⅛ t. salt
4 T. flour

1½ C. milk
4 T. butter
1 t. vanilla

Mix and cook until thick in double boiler.

Mrs. Atlee J. Miller

Rice Krispie Pie

3 eggs
½ C. brown sugar
¼ t. salt
1 C. light Karo

1 t. vanilla
2 T. butter, melted
1 C. Rice Krispies

Beat eggs. Add remaining ingredients. Pour into unbaked pie shell. Bake at 350°. Makes 1 pie.

Mrs. William Kuhns

127

Pecan Pie

10 eggs
3¼ C. brown sugar
2¾ C. light Karo
5 T. flour

1¼ C. cold water
5 T. butter
2 C. nuts

Beat eggs well and add remaining ingredients. Bake in 3 unbaked pastry shells at 375° until top is firm.

Mrs. Dan C. Yoder

Pecan Pie

3 eggs, slightly beaten
½ C. brown sugar
1 C. light corn syrup with
   a little water added
1 T. flour

1 T. butter, melted
½ t. salt
1 C. pecans or walnuts
1 t. vanilla

Mix all together and add 1 C. pecans or walnuts last. Put in unbaked pie crust and bake as you would for custard pie. Bake about 45 minutes.

Mrs. Adam Yoder
Mrs. Albert A. Raber, Jr.

Pecan Pie

3 eggs, beaten
¾ C. brown & white sugar
   (half and half)
½ T. flour
¾ C. Karo (½ light
   and ½ dark)

¼ C. water
¼ C. rolled oats
pinch of salt
1 t. vanilla
1 T. butter
½ C. chopped nuts

Beat eggs and add remaining ingredients. Bake at 350° in unbaked pie shell till top is firm.

Mrs. Dennis B. Miller

Raisin Cream Pie

1 C. cooked raisins
2 C. milk
1/2 C. brown sugar
1/2 C. white sugar

2 egg yolks, beaten
6 T. flour
1 T. butter

Cook till thick. Last add raisins and butter. Put in a baked pie crust.

Mrs. Roman E. Raber

Sour Cream Raisin Pie

3 eggs
1 C. sugar
1 1/2 C. sour cream

3 T. cornstarch
1 C. milk
3/4 C. boiled raisins, drained

Beat egg yolks only. Mix with milk, sour cream, sugar and cornstarch. Stir over medium heat until thick. Add boiled, drained raisins. Pour mixture into baked pie crust. Top with meringue or whipped cream. Makes one small pie.

Mrs. Melvin E. Shetler

Chocolate Mocha Pie

Dissolve 1 T. gelatine in 1/4 C. cold water. Combine in saucepan:

1 T. cocoa
1 t. coffee
1/8 t. salt
1 t. vanilla

3/4 C. sugar
1 1/4 C. milk
1 C. cream

Mix together cocoa, coffee, salt, sugar and milk. Bring to a boil, stirring constantly. Remove from heat and add gelatine. Cool till slightly thickened. Beat the cooked mixture until smooth. Beat cream. Add vanilla. Fold whipped cream into cooked mixture. Pour into 9" baked pie shell and top with nuts.

Mrs. Alfred M. Yoder
Ella A. Troyer

Pecan Pie

3 eggs
1 C. dark Karo
1/2 C. light Karo
1 t. vanilla

1/4 t. salt
2 T. butter
1 T. flour
1 C. nuts

Beat eggs, add remaining ingredients. Bake at 350° for 40 minutes.

Mrs. Henry E. Mast

Butterscotch Pecan Pie

1 C. light Karo
3/4 C. evaporated milk
1 egg, slightly beaten

3 oz. box instant vanilla
pudding
1 C. chopped pecans

Pastry dough for 8" pie. Blend Karo with pudding mix in bowl. Add evaporated milk and egg, stirring to blend. Add pecans and pour in pie shell. Bake at 375° for 45 minutes or until pie is set. Serve with whipped cream or plain.

Mrs. Henry E. Mast

Marshmallow Pie

20 marshmallows
1/2 C. milk

1 C. whipped cream
1/2 C. ground sweet
chocolate

Heat marshmallows and milk in double boiler until marshmallows are melted. Cool. Add whipped cream and chocolate. Fill a baked pie crust. Sprinkle top with a little chocolate.

Mrs. Henry E. Mast

Fruit Pie

1 C. water
1 C. sugar
1 C. 7-Up or Sprite

2 T. clear jel
3 oz. box jello

Add whatever fruit you wish. Don't add sugar to the fruit. Fill baked pie shell. Serve.

Mrs. Henry E. Mast

Rhubarb Cream Pie

2 T. flour
1 C. white sugar
2 egg yolks

½ C. sweet milk
2 C. rhubarb

Mix together and pour in unbaked pie shell. Bake at 425° till rhubarb is tender and filling is set. Beat egg whites. Add 3 T. brown sugar. Put over pie and bake till brown. Makes 1 pie.

Mrs. Henry M. Troyer
Mrs. Henry D. Miller

Rhubarb Orange Cream Pie

3 eggs, separated
1¼ C. sugar
¼ C. soft butter
3 T. frozen orange juice

¼ C. flour
¼ t. salt
2½ C. rhubarb
⅓ C. chopped pecans

Beat egg whites until stiff. Add ¼ C. sugar gradually, beating well after each addition. Add butter and orange concentrate to egg yolks, beat thoroughly. Add remaining 1 C. sugar, flour and salt. Beat well. Add rhubarb and stir well. Gently fold in meringue. Pour into pastry lined pan. Sprinkle with nuts. Bake at 375° for 15 minutes, reduce heat to 325° and bake 45-50 minutes or until done.

Mary Esta Yoder

Rhubarb Custard Pie

4½ C. white sugar
6 T. flour
12 T. Carnation milk

5 eggs, beaten
6 C. diced rhubarb

Mix, pour into unbaked pie shell and bake at 425° for 12 minutes then reduce heat to 325° for approximately 40 minutes. Makes 3 pies.

Mary Ellen Troyer

Rhubarb Custard Pie

4 C. rhubarb, cut fine
1½ C. sugar
⅛ t. salt
¼ t. nutmeg

1½ t. flour
3 eggs
⅔ C. rich milk

Beat eggs, add rest of ingredients, adding rhubarb last. Bake with a lattice crust on top. Bake at 325° for 40 minutes.

Mrs. Andy A. Yoder

Maple Nut Pie

Heat: ½ C. milk and 1 C. maple syrup

Add: 2 slightly beaten egg yolks. Cook a little, then add 1 T. gelatine, softened in a little cold water. Add 1 t. maple flavoring. Chill until mixture begins to thicken. Add 2 stiffly beaten egg whites. Add 1 C. whipped cream and ½ C. chopped nutmeats. Pour into pie shell. If you double this recipe it makes three 8" pies.

Mrs. Jonas A.M. Yoder
Mrs. Albert A. Raber, Jr.

Hickory Nut Pie

3 C. white sugar
2¼ C. light Karo
5 T. flour
1 C. cold water

5 T. butter, melted
2½ C. hickory nuts
10 eggs, beaten

Beat eggs. Add remaining ingredients. Pour in unbaked pie shell. Bake at 350° for 40 minutes. Makes 3 large pies.

Mrs. Dan Erb

Toasty Pecan Pie

1 C. white syrup
½ C. white sugar
3 eggs

1 t. vanilla
¼ t. salt
1 C. nuts

Combine syrup, sugar, eggs, vanilla and salt. Mix well. Add nuts. Pour in unbaked pie shell and bake at 350° for 50 minutes or until done.

Coconut Macaroon Pie

³/₄ C. white sugar
³/₄ C. brown sugar
¹/₂ C. softened oleo
2 eggs

¹/₃ C. flour
2 C. milk
1¹/₂ C. coconut

Beat together sugars and eggs. Add oleo and flour, blend well. Add milk. Fold in 1 C. coconut. Pour into unbaked pie shell. Top with ¹/₂ C. coconut. Bake at 300° for 1 hour. A double batch makes 3 pies.

Mrs. William Kuhns

Chocolate Chiffon Pie

1 T. gelatine
¹/₄ C. cold water
¹/₂ C. white sugar
2 T. cocoa
¹/₂ C. hot milk

¹/₂ C. light coffee
¹/₂ t. salt
1 t. vanilla
1 C. whipped cream

Soak gelatine in cold water 5 minutes. Boil sugar, cocoa, hot milk, coffee and salt. Add gelatine to this mixture, stirring thoroughly. Allow to cool. Add vanilla as mixture begins to thicken. Fold in whipped cream. Put in baked pie shell. Makes 1 large pie.

Mrs. Daniel Barkman

Chocolate Chiffon Pie

1¹/₂ C. milk
³/₄ C. white sugar

¹/₈ t. salt
1¹/₂ T. cocoa (scant)

Bring to a boil. Add:
1 T. gelatine, soaked in ¹/₄ C. cold water

Let set to jel slightly. Add:
1 C. whipped cream   1 t. vanilla

Pour into baked pie shells. Makes 2 pies.

Mrs. William Kuhns

Ground Cherry Pie

1½-2 C. ground cherries
1¼ C. brown sugar
pinch of salt

1 T. ReaLemon juice
    or vinegar
1 T. butter

Put cherries in saucepan. Add enough water to cover cherries. Add ReaLemon juice, brown sugar and salt. Bring to a boil. Thicken with clear jel. Turn down heat and boil for 2 minutes. Take off stove and add butter. Pour into unbaked pie shell. Put crust on top and bake at 450° until golden brown.

Anna Kay Bowman

Ground Cherry Pie

1 C. water
    Cook until soft.

2 C. ground cherries

1¾ C. sugar
3½ T. clear jel

1 C. water
2 T. butter

Mix sugar, water and clear jel. Cook a few minutes and add butter. Makes 2 pies.

Mrs. Jonas N. Borntrager

Strawberry Pie

Boil for 3 minutes:
¾ C. sugar
1½ C. water

1 T. cornstarch

Stir in one small box strawberry jello. Let cool but not set. Put 1 qt. fresh berries in baked pie shell. Pour cooled sauce over berries. Refrigerate for a couple hours. Top with Cool Whip and serve.

Mrs. Henry M. Troyer

134

Strawberry Pie

1 C. water   3 T. clear jel
1 C. 7-Up

Boil this together and add 1 (3 oz.) box strawberry jello. Cool a little then add 2 C. fresh sliced strawberries.

Katie Troyer

Fried Apple Pies

5 C. all-purpose flour   1 t. sugar
1 t. baking powder   1 C. Crisco
2 eggs, slightly beaten   13 oz. can evaporated
1 t. salt   milk

Cut shortening into dry ingredients. Mix eggs and milk together then add to first mixture. Mix with fork till it holds together (no more). Roll out rather thin. Cut out small rounds using a small saucer as a pattern. Put a spoonful of your favorite fruit pie filling on one side. Be sure your filling is fairly thick and cold. Fold over and seal edges well. Fry in deep fat until golden brown on both sides then glaze. Should make about 36 pies.

Mrs. Marlin Yoder

Shoestring Apple Pie

2½ C. white sugar   ¼ C. water
2 T. flour   4 C. finely diced apples
3 eggs, beaten

Sprinkle with cinnamon and dot with butter. Bake at 450° for 15 minutes. Reduce heat to 350°. Bake till the apples are soft. Makes two 9" pies.

Mrs. Levi J. Yoder

135

Apple Pie

1 C. brown sugar
1 C. water

   Boil then add:

1 T. clear jel with a little water
1 t. ReaLemon
1/2 t. salt
pinch of cinnamon
4 C. coarse shredded apples

   Cool. Put in unbaked pie crust. Top with another crust or crumbs. Bake at 450°.

Mrs. Viola Miller

Apple Pie

2 qt. pan 3/4 full of apple chunks
1 t. cinnamon
1 C. water

1 1/2 C. white sugar
1 t. allspice

   Thicken with 1 T. clear jel.

Edna Troyer

Caramel Pie

1 C. brown sugar
1 1/2 C. sweet milk
2 T. flour

1 egg
1 t. vanilla

   Mix all together and cook in a double boiler until thick.

Mrs. Fannie Yoder

Oatmeal Pie Crust

1 C. rolled oats
1/3 C. sifted flour

1/3 C. brown sugar
1/4 t. salt

Combine the above ingredients then cut in 1/3 C. butter till crumbly. Grease pie pan. Press crumbs on bottom and sides of pie pan. Bake at 350° for 15 minutes or till light brown.

Mrs. David D. Miller

Fresh Fruit Pie Filling

1 C. water
1 C. 7-Up

1 C. sugar
2 T. clear jel

Bring this to a boil and add 1 box of your favorite jello and whatever fresh fruit you choose.

Lizzie Raber

Lemon Pie

2 C. boiling water
2 T. cornstarch or clear jel
1 C. sugar

2 eggs
rind of 1/2 lemon and
  juice of 1 lemon
1 T. butter

Mix cornstarch and sugar. Slowly add boiling water, stirring constantly. Cook until mixture thickens. Remove from heat and add beaten egg yolks, butter, lemon rind and juice. Cook 1 minute. Pour into baked pastry crust. Top with meringue or whipped cream.

Mrs. John A. Weaver

Sponge Lemon Pie

1 C. sugar (scant)
1 T. flour
1 lemon

2 egg yolks
1 C. milk

Add grated rind and juice of 1 lemon. Beat whites of two eggs stiffly and stir in last. Bake slowly.

Mrs. Lloyd Miller

Vanilla Crumb Pie

½ C. brown sugar (packed)
1 T. flour
¼ C. light Karo

1½ t. vanilla
1 C. water
1 egg, beaten

Cook this over medium heat, stirring until mixture comes to a boil. Let cool.

1 C. flour
½ C. brown sugar (packed)
½ t. cream of tartar

½ t. soda
⅛ t. salt
¼ C. butter

Mix this until crumbly. Pour cooled mixture into pie shell. Top with crumbs. Bake at 350° for 40 minutes or until golden brown.

Mrs. Mose M. Miller

Rice Krispie Pie

5 eggs
pinch of salt
1 t. vanilla

¾ C. white sugar
1½ C. Karo
1 C. Rice Krispies

Beat eggs. Add remaining ingredients. Bake at 350° for about 1 hour.

Mrs. Dennis B. Miller

Rice Krispie Pie

4 eggs
1½ C. light Karo
1 t. vanilla
¼ t. salt
2 T. butter

2 T. water
2 T. brown sugar
1 T. flour
1 C. Rice Krispies

Beat eggs. Add remaining ingredients. Bake at 350° for 1 hour. Pour into unbaked pie crust.

Mrs. Aden Chupp

Apple Filling for Pie

12 C. grated apples
5 C. white sugar

3 C. water
6 T. minute tapioca

Mix together. Filling for 5-6 pies. Cold pack 15 minutes. Don't make jars too full. If using apples right away, cook 1 minute.

Topping for One Pie

1 C. quick rolled oats
1/3 C. chopped nuts
1/3 C. melted oleo

1/3 C. brown sugar
1/2 t. cinnamon

Mix and sprinkle on top of pie before baking. Put in baked pie shell and bake.

Mrs. Albert M.L. Yoder

Peach Pie

6 peaches, sliced
1 unbaked pie shell
1/4 C. flour

3/4 C. sugar
1 C. sweet cream

Arrange peaches in pie shell. Mix flour, sugar and cream. Pour over peaches. Top with crumbs.

Topping

1/3 C. flour
1/3 C. sugar

3 T. butter

Combine and put over first mixture. Bake at 425° for 10 minutes. Lower heat to 350° and bake until custard is set (approx. 30 minutes).

Fannie Miller

Peach Crumb Pie

2 1/2 T. minute tapioca
3/4 C. white sugar
1/4 t. salt

4 C. fresh sliced peaches
1 T. lemon juice

Mix and let stand for 5 minutes. Put in 9" pie shell.

Crumb Topping

1/3 C. brown sugar
1/4 C. flour

1/2 t. cinnamon
2 1/2 T. soft butter

Mix until crumbly. Put on top of peach pie filling.

Mrs. Henry M. Troyer

Peach Pie

4¼ C. water
1½ C. sugar
3 oz. box peach jello

⅔ C. clear jel
pinch of salt
2 T. butter

Cook together. Then add 4 C. fresh peach slices. Bring to boiling point. Makes 3 pies.

Mrs. Jonas N. Borntrager

Custard Pie

¾ C. brown sugar
1 T. flour
3 eggs

2½ C. milk
vanilla

Heat milk and beat the egg whites and put in last. Bake at 375° 10 minutes then at 350° until done.

Mrs. Adam Yoder

Velvet Custard Pie

Soak 1½ envelopes gelatine.
Heat 6 C. milk to scalding. Add gelatine and the following:
6 egg yolks
1 C. brown sugar
½ C. white sugar or to suit taste
vanilla

Beat egg whites and add last. This makes 2 large pies. Bake like other custard pies.

Mrs. Eli D. Miller

Pie Filler Apples to Can

12 C. shredded apples
5 C. white sugar

3 C. water
6 T. minute tapioca

Mix and cold pack 15 minutes. Do not make jars too full. Add cinnamon before baking.

Mrs. Jonas J. Miller

Vanilla Tart Pie

First Part:
1 C. dark Karo
1 C. white sugar

2 C. cold water
1 t. vanilla

Second Part:
1 C. white sugar
1 C. brown sugar
½ C. butter
½ C. buttermilk

½ C. sour cream
2 eggs
2 t. soda
2 C. flour

Put first part in bottom of pie pan and second on top. Makes 3 pies. Bake at 350°.

Mrs. Albert A. Raber, Jr.

Oatmeal Nut Pie

2 eggs, beaten
⅔ C. oatmeal (quick)
⅔ C. white sugar
⅔ C. nuts

1 t. vanilla
2 t. oleo
½ C. brown sugar
½ C. light Karo
½ C. milk

Beat eggs. Add rest of ingredients. Pour into an unbaked pie shell. Bake at 375°.

Mrs. Paul E. Miller

Pumpkin Custard Pie

1 C. cooked pumpkin
3 eggs, separated
1 T. flour
¼ C. brown sugar
½ C. white sugar

½ t. salt
½ t. cinnamon
¾ t. pumpkin pie spice
2 C. milk, scalded

Mix ingredients in order given. Fold in beaten egg whites last. Pour in unbaked pie shell and bake at 450° for 5 minutes then at 325° for 40 minutes or till done.

Mary Esta Yoder

Pumpkin Pie

4 eggs, separated
1 C. white sugar
1 C. brown sugar
2 C. pumpkin
2 t. pumpkin pie spice

4 T. flour
pinch of salt
2 t. vanilla
5 C. milk (I use 1-2 cans
  Pet milk)-heat

Beat egg whites then beat egg yolks and brown sugar together till light in color. Add white sugar then rest of ingredients. Fold egg whites in last. Bake at 425° till brown then at 325° for 45 minutes or till done. Yield: 2 pies.

Mrs. J. L. Miller

Fresh Peach Pie

Cook together:
2½ C. water
½ C. white sugar
3 oz. box peach jello

1 heaping T. plus 1 level
  T. clear jel
2 ripe peaches, sliced

Pour into a baked pie shell. Top with whipped cream when ready to eat.

Mrs. Henry D. Miller

Peach Custard Pie

2-3 peaches
1½ C. scalded milk
¾ C. white sugar

¼ t. salt
2 eggs
2 T. flour

Slice peaches in unbaked crust. Sprinkle with ¼ C. sugar. Mix flour, salt, ½ C. sugar and egg yolks slowly. Add hot milk then pour over peaches and bake till custard is set. Whip the egg whites and add 4 T. sugar. Put on pie. Return to oven till brown. Bake at 350°.

Mrs. Levi A. Hershberger

Crumb Pie

2 C. brown sugar
2 eggs
2 C. light Karo

1 pt. water
3 T. flour
1 t. vanilla

Cook and cool. Pour in pie shell.

Crumbs

2 C. flour
½ C. butter or lard

1 t. soda
1 t. cream of tartar

Put the crumbs on top of pie and bake till brown.

Mrs. Fannie Yoder
Mrs. Henry M. Troyer

Apple Goodie

1½ C. sugar
pinch of salt
1½ qt. sliced apples

2 T. flour
1 t. cinnamon

Top Part:
1 C. oatmeal
1 C. flour
⅓ t. baking powder

1 C. brown sugar
¼ t. soda
⅔ C. butter

Mix sugar, flour, salt and cinnamon. Add to apples and mix. Put in bottom of greased pan. Mix ingredients of top part until crumbly. Put on apples and bake till brown. Serve with milk.

Ada J. Yoder

Pie Dough

2¼ C. lard
2 t. baking powder
1 T. vinegar

1½ t. salt
6 C. flour

Put 1 T. vinegar in 1 C. and fill up with hot water. Pour over lard and let stand until soft. Stir in flour (part whole wheat if you wish), baking powder and salt. Set in cold place overnight. Enough for approximately 6 pies.

Mrs. Emma Hershberger

- Notes -

Salads

Taco Salad

1 med. head lettuce
8 oz. shredded cheddar cheese
1 lg. onion, chopped
1 pkg. taco seasoning

1 lb. hamburger
1 small can kidney beans
4 med. tomatoes, diced
1 pkg. taco flavored chips

Fry hamburger, add taco seasoning, reserving 1 T. for dressing. Cut lettuce and add all other ingredients except chips.

Dressing

8 oz. Thousand Island dressing
$1/2$ C. sugar
1 T. taco seasoning
1 T. taco sauce

When ready to serve add dressing and chips.

Mrs. Emanuel Weaver
Mrs. Emanuel H. Yoder

Taco Salad

1 med. head lettuce, chopped
1 lb. hamburger
8 oz. cheddar cheese
1 large onion, chopped
4 med. tomatoes
1 pkg. taco chips
1 pkg. taco seasoning

Dressing

8 oz. Thousand Island dressing
$1/3$ C. white sugar
1 T. taco seasoning
1 T. taco sauce

Brown hamburger, add taco seasoning, reserving 1 T. for dressing. Start with lettuce and end with cheese. Toss with chips and dressing.

Mrs. Abe E. Mast
Mrs. John J. Troyer

Ribbon Salad

6 oz. pkg. lemon jello
6 oz. pkg. lime jello
6 oz. pkg. raspberry jello
6 C. boiling water
2 C. miniature marshmallows

3 C. cold water
8 oz. cream cheese
¼ C. Miracle Whip
2 C. whipped topping
20 oz. crushed pineapple

Dissolve jello flavors separately, using 2 C. boiling water for each. Stir marshmallows into lemon jello. Add 1½ C. cold water to lime jello and pour into an oblong pan. Chill until set. Add 1½ C. cold water to raspberry jello and set aside at room temperature. Then add cream cheese to lemon mixture, beat until blended. Chill until slightly thickened, then blend in Miracle Whip, whipped topping and pineapple. Chill until thickened then gently spoon over lime jello. Chill until set. Meanwhile chill raspberry jello until slightly thickened then pour over lemon mixture. Chill until firm.

Katie Coblentz
Mrs. Aden Chupp
Mrs. Henry N. Miller
Mrs. Mose E. Hershberger

Ribbon Salad

Layer 1:
Prepare 3 oz. box red jello according to directions. Pour into 8" x 8" pan.

Layer 2:
1 small can crushed pineapple
⅔ C. milk
16 marshmallows
8 oz. cream cheese

3 oz. box lemon jello
1 C. whipping cream
⅔ C. nuts

Heat milk, marshmallows and cheese in double boiler until melted. Add lemon jello. Cool and add pineapple, nuts and whipped cream. Pour over layer of red jello after it has set. Chill.

Layer 3:
Prepare orange jello according to directions and pour on top. Let set until firm.

Mrs. Levi H. Mast

Finger Jello

5 pkg. Knox gelatine
2 (6 oz.) pkg. jello (any kind)

2½ C. boiling water
¼ C. white sugar

Put gelatine in 2 C. cold water. Let set. Put jello and ¼ C. sugar in bowl. Add 2½ C. boiling water. Add gelatine. Stir until everything is dissolved. Add 1 C. cold water. Pour into a pan. Let set and serve.

Mrs. Henry D. Miller

Ribbon Salad

Bottom:
3 oz. pkg. green jello
1 small can crushed pineapples
½ C. nuts

Center:
1 pkg. yellow jello
8 oz. cream cheese
Mix together when cool. Add ¾ C. whipped cream.

Top:
1 pkg. red jello

Let each layer set before adding the next.

Mrs. Henry E. Schlabach

Coleslaw Dressing

5 T. sugar
1 T. plus 1 t. flour
1 t. dry mustard
pinch of salt
1 egg, beaten

¼ C. vinegar
¾ C. water
¼ C. butter
1 C. salad dressing

Thoroughly mix sugar, flour, mustard, salt and egg. Set aside. Combine vinegar, water and butter. Bring to a boil. Add first mixture and cook a few minutes. Remove from heat. Beat well. Add salad dressing and beat again. Will keep in refrigerator for several weeks.

Mary Esta Yoder

Under the Sea Salad

Bottom Layer:

6 oz. box lime jello   1 can crushed pineapple,
½ C. nuts   drained

Prepare jello following directions on box. When partly set add pineapple and nuts. Put in bottom of pan. Chill.

Center Layer:

6 oz. box lemon jello   8 oz. cream cheese,
¾ C. whipping cream   softened

Prepare jello. Whip cream. Add cream cheese. Add cream cheese and cream mixture to partly set jello. Pour on top of completely set lime jello.

Top Layer:

6 oz. box jello

Prepare jello. Pour on top of completely set lemon jello. Chill until completely set.

Clara Yoder
Mrs. William Kuhns

7-Up Salad

1 box lemon jello
1 box lime jello
2 C. hot water to dissolve

Add 2 C. 7-Up. When jello is set a little add:

1 can crushed pineapple
1 C. nuts
½ pkg. small marshmallows

Let this set to harden.

Topping: 3 oz. box strawberry jello and 1 C. hot water.

When jello is set a little, add 1 C. whipped cream and 1 3 oz. pkg. cream cheese. Beat until smooth and slightly thickened. Put on top of jello and let set.

Mrs. Raymond D. Miller

149

Frozen Tropical Fruit Salad

2 C. white sugar
3 C. warm water
1 (6 oz.) can frozen orange juice (prepare as directed)
1 #2 can crushed pineapple
8 bananas, sliced

Mix together and freeze several hours. Serve partially frozen.

Ada Weaver

Dressing For Tossed Salad

2 C. salad oil
2 C. salad dressing
1 1/2 C. white sugar
1 C. Wesson oil

1/8 C. vinegar
1/8 C. mustard
1/2 t. celery seed
pinch of salt

Mix together using beater.

Mrs. Viola Miller

Pineapple Cool Whip Salad

Mix 1 C. white sugar and 20 oz. can pineapple. In saucepan combine 6 T. water and 2 pkg. Knox gelatine. Bring to a boil and pour over pineapple mixture and stir. Set in refrigerator.

Prepare:
2 med. carrots
1 C. chopped celery
1 C. cottage cheese

1 C. nuts
1 lg. Cool Whip
1 1/2 C. mayonnaise

Mix with first mixture and let set.

Ada Burkholder

Potato Salad

Peel and cook a 6 qt. kettle of potatoes. Put through Salad Master. Let cool. Put through finest Salad Master. Cook 12 eggs and mash with potato masher. Add ½ med. onion, chopped fine, and 1½ C. celery, cut fine.

Dressing

3 C. salad dressing
4 C. white sugar
½ C. milk

¼ C. vinegar
6 T. prepared mustard
2 t. salt

Fix and mix a few days ahead. Keep chilled.

Mrs. William Kuhns

24 Hour Potato Salad

12 C. potatoes, cooked with skins
12 hard-boiled eggs
½ C. onions, or less to suit taste
2 C. celery, finely chopped
3 C. salad dressing
6 T. mustard (prepared)
2 t. salt
2½ C. white sugar
¼ C. vinegar

Put potatoes through a Salad Master when cooled. Mash 1 egg at a time with potato masher. Press only once. Mix all ingredients together. Will keep 4-5 days.

Mary Schlabach
Mrs. Adam Yoder
Mrs. John J. Troyer
Mrs. Emanuel Weaver
Mrs. David E. Hershberger

Potato Salad

12 med. potatoes, cooked
11 hard-boiled eggs
1 C. celery, cut fine
1 small onion
1 C. macaroni, chopped
    Put eggs and potatoes through Salad Master. Mix all together.

1½ C. Miracle Whip
½ C. vinegar
3 t. mustard
1½ C. white sugar

Blend together and mix with potatoes. Refrigerate. Best flavor when mixed one day before using.

Mrs. Junior A. Yoder

Potato Salad

Cook potatoes whole (add salt). Not too soft. Put through Salad Master.
12 C. cooked potatoes
12 hard-boiled eggs, cut up
½ med. onion, cut fine
1½ C. celery, cut fine
carrots (optional)

Sauce (do not heat):
3 C. salad dressing
6 t. mustard
¼ C. vinegar

2½ C. white sugar
4 t. salt
½ C. milk

Blend together and mix with potatoes.

Mrs. Nelson A. Barkman

Potato Salad

6 C. cooked potatoes
6 or more eggs
1/2 C. onion
1 C. celery
1/2 C. salad dressing

1 C. white sugar
3 T. mustard
2 T. vinegar
1 T. salt
1/4 C. milk

Put potatoes and eggs through grinder. Has a better flavor if put together the day before.

Mrs. Henry D. Miller
Ada Burkholder

Lettuce Dressing

1 qt. Miracle Whip
1/2 bottle Sweet-n-Sour dressing
3 cans Milnot milk
3 t. salt

1/2 bottle French dressing
4 C. sugar
2 T. mustard
vinegar if necessary

Combine all ingredients and beat well. Makes one gallon.

Mrs. Nelson A. Barkman
Mrs. Albert M. Yoder

Cottage Cheese Salad

1 pt. small curd cottage cheese
1 small box orange jello (dry)
9 oz. Cool Whip
1 small can crushed pineapple, drained
1 can mandarin oranges, drained

Mix together and chill.

Mrs. Henry E. Schlabach
Mrs. Nelson A. Barkman

7 Layer Salad

1½ head lettuce
1 med. onion
15 oz. frozen peas

1 lb. bacon
¾ lb. grated cheese
8 hard-boiled eggs

Put in layers as listed. Put dressing on when ready to serve.

Dressing

¾ C. Miracle Whip
½ C. sugar
¼ C. milk

Blend together.

Mrs. Andy A. Yoder

Potato Salad

12 C. potatoes, cooked and diced
12 eggs
1 C. shredded carrots

½ med. onion
1½ C. chopped celery

Dressing

3 C. salad dressing
7 T. prepared mustard
½ C. milk

2 t. salt
2½ C. white sugar

Blend together and mix with potatoes.

Mrs. Marlin Yoder

Overnight Salad

1 head lettuce, chopped
5-6 pieces celery, cut up
1 (15 oz.) pkg. frozen peas, cooked, drained and cooled
1 lg. onion, minced
1 layer bacon, fried, drained and broken up
1 layer shredded cheddar cheese
1 pt. mayonnaise
½ C. white sugar

Spread mayonnaise over top and sprinkle with sugar. Let set overnight in refrigerator. Toss just before serving.

Mrs. William Byler

7 Layer Salad

1 head lettuce	1 C. celery
4 eggs, diced	1 pkg. frozen peas (10 oz.),
1/2 C. peppers	uncooked
1 onion	chipped chopped ham

Cover with 2 C. salad dressing. Sprinkle with 2 T. brown sugar and 4 oz. shredded cheddar cheese.

Mrs. Roman E. Raber

Potato Salad Dressing

3 C. salad dressing	2 1/2 C. white sugar
6 T. prepared mustard	1/4 C. vinegar
2 t. salt	1/2 C. Milnot milk

Blend together.

Mrs. Mose M. Miller

Potato Salad

12 C. cooked diced potatoes	1 1/2 C. celery
1 1/2 med. onion	1 C. shredded carrots
12 eggs, cooked	1 can navy beans

Dressing for Salad

3 C. salad dressing	2 1/2 C. sugar
3 T. mustard	4 t. salt
1/4 C. vinegar	1/2 C. milk

Blend together and mix with potatoes. Makes 3 1/2 qts. Make a day ahead.

Mrs. Daniel Barkman

Sauerkraut

Shred cabbage and weigh 5 lbs. Measure 3 T. pure granulated salt and sprinkle over 5 lbs. shredded cabbage. Allow to stand a few minutes to wilt slightly. Mix well and pack in container very firmly with potato masher so juices will just cover cabbage. Place a water filled plastic bag on top of cabbage. This fits snugly against the cabbage and sides of container and prevents exposure to air. Keep at room temperature (68°-72°). Fermentation is usually completed in 5-6 weeks.

To store: Heat sauerkraut to simmering. Do not boil. Pack hot sauerkraut into clean, hot jars and cover with hot juice to ½" from top of jar. Adjust lids. Process in boiling water bath 15 minutes for pints and 20 minutes for quarts. Start to count processing time as soon as hot jars are placed into the boiling water.

Mrs. David D. Miller

Sauerkraut

Shred cabbage. To each quart add 1 heaping T. salt. Mix with hands. Pack firmly in jars. Add ½ T. sugar and 1 T. vinegar to each quart. Add boiling water. Use butter knife up through cabbage so water goes through cabbage. Seal tightly. Do not cold pack. Store in cool dark place. Set jars on paper as juice will leak out of jars. Ready in 6-8 weeks.

Edna Troyer

How to Make Sauerkraut

Shred cabbage then scald with boiling water. Let stand till cool. Drain and press out water as good as you can. Next put a layer of cabbage in a crock and put some salt on. Take a wooden masher and mash it down. Add another layer of cabbage and salt and mash it down again. Do this till the cabbage is all in crock. Put large cabbage leaves on top and cover with a white cloth. Press down, keeping water on too. Let stand 2 weeks. Cold pack 3 hours. Don't put any water in jars. Ready to eat.

Mary Ann N. Coblentz

To Make Sauerkraut

Cut cabbage up fine and pack in jars. Add 1 t. salt, 1 t. sugar and 1 C. warm water. Seal jars. Will be ready to use in 3 weeks. Will not completely seal but will keep for years that way. Delicious.

Fannie Miller

Sauerkraut

Shred cabbage and put in jars. To 1 qt. cabbage add 1 t. salt, 1 t. sugar and ³/₄ C. warm water. Close jars and let set in cool dark place 3 weeks or so, then cold pack 1 hour.

Mrs. William Kuhns

Green Salad

3 oz. lime jello
3 oz. lemon jello

Dissolve the above in 2 C. hot water and add a No. 2 can crushed pineapple, with the juice. Cool. When this gets syrupy add:

1 pt. cottage cheese
1 can Eagle Brand milk

1 C. mayonnaise
¹/₂ C. chopped nuts

Mrs. Viola Miller

Overnight Leaf Salad

1 head lettuce, cut up
1 head cauliflower, cut up
1 sweet onion, cut up
¹/₂ C. shredded carrots

1 lb. fried bacon
2 C. mayonnaise
¹/₃ C. Parmesan cheese
¹/₄ C. sugar

Put in layers in order given and refrigerate overnight. Toss just before serving.

Mary Esta Yoder

Corn Salad

1 head cabbage
2 bunches celery
1 doz. ears of corn

Cook cabbage, celery and corn then drain. Add:

1 C. vinegar
3 C. water
2 C. white sugar
1 t. mustard seed
2 t. celery seed
4 t. salt
2 onions
1 red and 1 yellow pepper

Heat to boiling point. Put in hot jars and seal.

Mrs. Fannie Yoder

Terrific Bacon Salad

½ med. head lettuce
⅓ C. chopped celery
1 C. grated cheese
1 C. frozen peas
1 lb. bacon, fried and cut up
2 hard-boiled eggs
6-8 radishes sliced thin
¾ C. mayonnaise

Place ingredients in layers starting with cut up lettuce. Add ½ of bacon pieces, then celery and radishes. Now add the frozen peas, slice the eggs and add to other layers. Top the eggs with rest of bacon pieces and cover with mayonnaise. To finish top with grated cheese. Refrigerate 6-8 hours before serving.

Mrs. Edwin M. Troyer

Orange Salad

2 pkg. Dream Whip or 1 large Cool Whip
1 C. commercial sour cream
½ pkg. miniature marshmallows
20 oz. can crushed pineapple, drained
17 oz. can fruit cocktail, drained
3 oz. box jello

Mix Dream Whip or Cool Whip. Add sour cream and stir in dry jello. Fold in fruit and marshmallows.

Mrs. Paul Frey

Orange Apricot Salad

2 pkg. orange jello
2 C. hot water
1 can drained crushed pineapple
1 can diced apricots, drained
1 C. mixed juice from the fruit

Mix and let set in a dish.

Topping

1 beaten egg   1/2 C. sugar
2 T. flour

Mix together. Add 1 C. juice and cook until thick. Add 2 T. butter and cool. When ready to serve, whip in 1 C. whipped cream and pour over the jello salad.

Mrs. Raymond D. Miller

Broccoli Salad

1 bundle fresh broccoli, cut up
1 medium onion, diced
2 C. grated sharp cheddar cheese
6 pieces bacon, fried and cut up
some cauliflower

Sauce

3/4 C. sour cream   1/2 C. sugar
3/4 C. mayonnaise   1/4 t. salt

Mix sauce ingredients and pour over broccoli mixture. Can be made a day ahead.

Mrs. David Beachy

Kraft Cheese

2½ gal. milk (let sour till thick). Heat until too hot to hold your hand in. Not boiling. Drain in organdy bag or cheesecloth. Squeeze out all water. To 4 C. curds add 1 t. soda and mix. Let stand 30 minutes. Put ⅓ C. butter in pan and melt. Put cheese in and stir constantly till cheese is all melted. Add 2 t. salt. If you want spreading cheese, add 1 C. milk or cream when melted.

Mrs. David D. Miller

Haystack

2 C. crushed soda crackers
2 C. rice, cooked in salt water
1 head lettuce, chopped
1 pkg. corn chips, crushed
6 diced tomatoes
6 hard-boiled eggs, mashed

Brown and drain 3 lbs. hamburger. Add 1 qt. Ragu spaghetti sauce and 1 qt. homemade spaghetti or pizza sauce, heated. Plenty of this makes it good. Mix 3 cans cheddar cheese soup with 2 cans milk. Heat. Pass in order given and put on one pile on plate. For nice fluffy rice, do not wash before cooking. Combine 2 C. rice and 4 C. cold water and 1 t. salt. Bring to hard boil, uncovered. Lower heat and cover with tight lid. Simmer 20 minutes. Do not stir.

Mrs. David D. Miller

Haystack

2 C. white cracker crumbs
2 C. rice, cooked
1 head lettuce, chopped

1 pkg. corn chips, crushed
6 diced tomatoes
1 C. chopped nuts

Brown 3 lb. hamburger and add 1 qt. Ragu sauce and 1 qt. pizza sauce. Plenty of this makes it good. Heat 3 cans cheddar cheese soup with 1½ cans milk. Pass in order given and put on 1 pile.

Mrs. Jonas J.D. Miller
Mrs. Levi H. Mast
Mrs. Henry D. Miller

Mrs. Paul Frey
Mrs. Delbert R. Troyer
Clara Yoder

Haystack

Prepare the following and set out in bowls.
4 C. crushed Club, Ritz or soda crackers
lettuce, chopped
onion, chopped
8-10 tomatoes
hard-boiled eggs, chopped
4 C. hot cooked rice or noodles
cheddar cheese, shredded
kidney beans, drained (hot or cold)

Brown 4 lb. ground beef and mix with 1 qt. spaghetti sauce and 1 pkg. hot taco seasoning. Heat 2 cans cheddar cheese soup diluted with 1½ C. milk. Pile ingredients on top of each other, beginning with crackers. Top with cheese soup and serve with taco sauce, shredded carrots, diced celery or chopped avocados if desired.

Mrs. John A. Weaver
Mrs. Joe Erb

Haystack

½ lb. saltine crackers, crushed
4 lb. hamburger with small chopped onion, fried
12 small tomatoes, diced
4 C. precooked minute rice
2 heads lettuce, chopped
1 big bag corn chips, crushed
2 jars Ragu sauce
4 cans cream of cheddar soup
2 cans milk
2 C. chopped onions

Brown hamburger in butter with onion. Add 2 jars Ragu sauce (we use our own pizza sauce). Heat 4 cans cream of cheddar soup diluted with 2 cans milk (we make our own soup with white sauce and add Velveeta cheese). Put on plate in order: crackers, rice, lettuce, corn chips, tomatoes, onions, hamburger sauce with soup on top in haystack fashion. Serves 14.

Mrs. William Kuhns

Straw Hats

Brown 1 lb. hamburger and onion. Add:
2 small cans pork and beans
1 small can chili beans
$1/3$ C. sugar
1 C. catsup
1 t. Worcestershire sauce
Add tomato juice for more liquid.
   Place in oven and heat. Order of stack:

corn chips, crushed
bean and hamburger mixture
lettuce
tomatoes, cubed
hot sauce

cucumbers
cheese, grated
catsup
mustard

   Slice and peel cucumbers. Add equal amounts of water, sugar and vinegar. Add a pinch of salt. Let set overnight.

Mrs. Lloyd Miller

Straw Hats

chili sauce
2 lb. hamburger, browned with onions
large can pork and beans
small can hot chili beans
ketchup - some tomato juice
brown sugar and salt to taste
2-3 T. Worcestershire sauce

   Stack on plate in order given:
crushed Dorito chips
chili sauce
shredded cheddar cheese
lettuce
diced tomatoes
cucumber slices

   Top with variety of different dressings (mild taco, French and Red Hot).

Clara Yoder

Instant Delight Salad

2 pkg. lemon jello
2 C. boiling water
2 C. cold water

3 bananas, diced
3 apples, diced
1-2 cans crushed pineapple

Dissolve jello in hot water then add cold water. Let cool. Add fruit and let set.

Topping

2 T. flour
1/2 C. sugar

1 egg
1 C. pineapple juice or
add water to make 1 C.

Blend sugar and flour. Add juice and egg. Beat until smooth and cook over low heat, stirring constantly, until thickened. Cool. Fold in 1 C. whipped cream, vanilla and sugar to taste. Spread on top of jello. Nuts may be added.

Mrs. Merlin Troyer

Haystack Dinner

Add on plate in order given:
cracker crumbs
baked beans
browned hamburger
cut up lettuce
boiled diced eggs
shredded carrots
shredded cheese
Sweet & Sour dressing
dried cubed bread

Sweet and Sour Dressing

1 C. white sugar
1/4 t. pepper
1 t. celery seed
3 t. prepared mustard

1 medium chopped onion
1 T. Miracle Whip
1/3 C. vinegar (if strong, add
water)

Slowly add 1 C. salad oil. We think this is the best haystack!

Emma Hershberger

Haystack

½ lb. soda crackers, crushed	1 lb. cheese, shredded
4 C. rice	1 lg. can kidney beans
2 head lettuce, chopped	2 pkg. corn chips
2 tomatoes, diced	4 lb. hamburger

Brown hamburger and add 2 large cans Ragu spaghetti sauce. Heat 3 cans cheddar cheese soup with 2 cans milk. I usually add Velveeta cheese too. Starting with crushed crackers on plate add rest of ingredients in order given to make haystack.

Lizzie Raber
Mrs. Henry E. Schlabach
Mrs. Adam Yoder
Ada Mae Raber

Trash Can Supper

Build a fire. A grate over concrete blocks is okay. Place following into a large trash can in following order:
36-48 ears of corn (cleaned) placed on end. Should cover entire bottom. 1 peck scrubbed new potatoes (medium size). 3 heads cabbage, quartered. 3 pkgs. scrubbed carrots, whole turnips or celery optional. 2 lb. green beans on sheet of foil. Salt and pepper. Add crumbled bacon. Place on top of everything else. Place 2 qt. hot water in trash can. Cover with lid and place on fire. Should be steaming in 30 minutes. Add hot dog or bologna about 45 minutes before serving. Add smoked sausage about 1 hour before serving. Fresh sausage should be precooked. This usually takes about 3 hours on medium fire. Serves 20-25 people.

Mary Ellen Troyer

Bacon Cheese Spread

2 (8 oz.) pkg. cream cheese	8 oz. sharp cheddar
10 slices bacon, fried and crumbled	½ C. mayonnaise
⅓ C. onion, chopped	1 T. lemon juice
½ green pepper, chopped	¼ t. garlic powder

Soften cream cheese at room temperature. Stir in remaining ingredients. Mix well. Serve with crackers.

Mrs. William Byler

164

Creamy Cabbage Slaw

6 C. shredded cabbage
¼ C. sliced green onion
1 C. salad dressing or mayonnaise
2 T. white sugar

2 T. vinegar
2 t. celery seed
1 t. salt

Combine shredded cabbage and onions and chill. Blend rest of ingredients, stir until sugar is dissolved. Chill. Toss lightly with cabbage mixture. Makes 10 servings.

Mrs. Jonas J. Miller

Sweet and Sour Carrots

2 lb. sliced carrots, cooked
1 onion, thinly sliced

1 green onion (optional)

Sauce

1 can cream of tomato soup
1 C. sugar
½ C. vegetable oil

½ C. vinegar
1 t. salt
1 t. dry mustard

Mix well. Bring to a boil. Pour over carrots. Serve hot or cold.

Mrs. Wyman D. Miller

Tossed Salad Dressing

1 C. Miracle Whip
1 C. Mazola oil
1 C. white sugar
⅓ C. chopped onion

¼ C. vinegar
½ t. salt
1 t. celery seed

Blend together.

Mrs. J.L. Miller

Salad Dressing

1/2 C. vinegar
1/2 C. water
1/2 C. milk
2 T. flour

2 eggs
1 T. mustard
3 T. sugar

Cook in double boiler and add salt and pepper to taste.

Miss Verna L. Miller

Sauce For Coleslaw or Potato Salad

2 C. salad dressing
3 T. mustard
1 T. vinegar

2 C. white sugar
2 t. salt
1/4 C. milk or cream

Combine ingredients and blend well.

Cauliflower Salad

1 head lettuce, cut up
1 head cauliflower, cut up
1 med. onion, chopped
1 lb. bacon, fried and broken in pieces

Put 2 C. Miracle Whip over top like frosting. Sprinkle 1/4 C. white sugar over Miracle Whip and add 2 C. shredded cheese on top. Let set overnight. When ready to use, drain water off and mix together.

French Dressing

2 t. minced onion
2 t. salt
1 C. white sugar
3/4 C. oil

1/3 C. vinegar
1 C. ketchup
1 t. paprika
juice of one lemon

Mix all together and beat in 1 T. mayonnaise.

Mrs. Noah L. Yoder

Sweet French Dressing

1 C. white sugar
1 C. salad oil
1/2 C. vinegar
3/4 C. catsup

pinch of salt
3 T. onion
1 t. celery seed

Blend together.

Mrs. David L. Troyer
Mrs. Nelson A. Barkman

Homemade French Dressing

2 C. Wesson oil
2 C. white sugar
3/4 C. vinegar

3/4 C. catsup
2 t. Worcestershire sauce
2 t. salt

Combine all ingredients and beat well.

Susie Hershberger

Thousand Island Dressing

3 C. salad dressing
3/8 C. catsup
3/8 C. relish

3/16 t. salt
1/2 C. white sugar

Put all ingredients together and mix.

Mrs. John A. Miller

Vegetable Dip

1 C. mayonnaise
1 C. sour cream
1 T. Beau Monde

1 T. dill weed
1 T. parsley flakes
1 T. onion flakes

Mix and enjoy.

Mary Ellen Troyer
Susie Hershberger

Good Vegetable Dip

1 pkg. Hidden Valley salad dressing mix (green pack)
2 C. mayonnaise
8 oz. plain yogurt

Mix all together. Good to eat with any raw vegetables and apples.

Mrs. Wyman D. Miller

Relish Dip

2 C. salad dressing
1 (8 oz.) cream cheese
1 small onion or onion flakes

2 T. Worcestershire sauce
3 beef bouillon cubes,
dissolve in hot water

Mix all together and store in refrigerator.

Mrs. Junior A. Yoder

Eat-N-House French Dressing

2 C. salad dressing
1 C. sugar
1/3 C. vinegar
1/3 C. catsup
1/2 t. salt
1/2 t. pepper

1/2 t. Worcestershire sauce
1/2 t. mustard
1/3 C. salad oil
1/2 t. paprika
chopped onion

Mix well. Half the recipe makes exactly 1 pint dressing. When using half the recipe 1/3 C. = 3 T.

Mary Esta Yoder

Cheese Ball

22 oz. cream cheese
1 t. salt
2 T. onions, finely chopped
2 T. Worcestershire sauce

1 t. onion salt
6 oz. Velveeta cheese
1 C. cheddar cheese

Mix all together and form into ball. Eat with your choice of crackers.

Mrs. Adam Yoder

Sweet and Sour Dressing

1 medium onion, finely chopped
1 C. vinegar
1/4 C. water
1 C. white sugar
1 t. salt

1 C. vegetable oil
1/4 t. black pepper
1 T. Miracle Whip
2 t. mustard
1 t. celery salt or seed

Beat all together with beater.

Mrs. Eli D. Miller
Mrs. Henry D. Miller
Mrs. Jonas N. Borntrager

Mrs. Jonas J. Miller
Edna Troyer
Mrs. Atlee J. Miller

Sweet-N-Sour Dressing

3 C. vinegar
6 C. white sugar
2 t. celery seed

1/2 t. salt
3 t. dry mustard
8 C. Wesson oil

Blend all ingredients together. This makes about 1 gallon.

Susie Hershberger

Cheese Ball

2 (8 oz.) cream cheese, softened
1 C. cheddar cheese
2 T. onion, chopped

2 T. Worcestershire sauce
1 T. lemon juice
1 T. parsley flakes

Mix together and set aside till cold. Form a ball and roll in English walnuts. Slice and spread on Ritz crackers.

Mrs. Emanuel H. Yoder
Mrs. John J. Troyer
Susie Hershberger
Mrs. Dannie H. Burkholder

Mrs. Abe J. Schlabach
Mrs. John A. Miller
Mrs. Mose E. Hershberger
Mrs. Albert M.L. Yoder

Cheese Ball

2 (8 oz.) pkg. Philadelphia cream cheese
1 squirt can cheddar cheese
small onion, diced fine
dash of Lawry's seasoning salt
nuts

Soften cream cheese and cream together with remaining ingredients except nuts. Shape into ball and roll in nuts. Refrigerate.

Ruth Ann Frey

Cheese Ball

3 (8 oz.) pkg. cream cheese
2 t. onion flakes
$1/4$ t. Accent

$1/4$ t. garlic salt
$1/4$ C. crushed pineapple
1 can dried beef

Soften cream cheese and blend with rest of ingredients. Shape into ball. Refrigerate. Delicious with any kind of crackers.

Mrs. Dannie H. Burkholder

L & K Dressing

1 C. salad dressing
1 C. Wesson oil (scant)
1 C. sugar

$1/4$ C. vinegar
1 chopped onion
celery (optional)

Beat well. Good for cabbage and lettuce.

Mrs. Mose M. Miller

Sweet-N-Sour Dressing

1 C. sugar
$1/4$ C. vinegar
1 T. salad dressing
$1/4$ t. pepper
1 medium onion

$1/4$ C. water
1 C. vegetable oil
2 t. mustard
1 t. salt
1 t. celery seed

Beat with egg beater.

Mrs. Nelson A. Barkman

- *Favorite Recipes* -

- Notes -

Main Dishes

Barbecued Hamburgers

1 lb. hamburger
1 C. soft bread crumbs
½ C. milk
salt and pepper to taste

Mix above mixture together. Form balls of mixture and brown in 2 T. fat. Place in baking dish and cover with following sauce:

2 T. sugar
2 T. vinegar

2 T. Worcestershire sauce
1 C. catsup

Cover and bake 30 minutes at 350°.

Mrs. Adam Yoder

Juicy Meat Loaf

2 lb. ground beef
2 eggs, well beaten
¾ C. tomato juice
¾ C. uncooked Quaker oats

¼ C. chopped onion
2 t. salt
¼ t. pepper

Combine all ingredients thoroughly. Pack firmly in loaf pan. Bake at 350° for 1 hour. If a sauce is desired mix 2 T. each of ketchup, mustard and brown sugar and spread over meat loaf before baking.

Mrs. Paul D. Shetler

Barbecued Hamburgers

2 lb. hamburger
2 eggs, slightly beaten
2 C. soft bread crumbs

2 t. salt
¼ C. minced onion
¼ C. milk

Combine all ingredients and mix well. Shape into thin patties. Broil over hot coals, brushing both sides with barbecue sauce.

Barbecue Sauce

2 T. brown sugar
2 T. vinegar

2 T. Worcestershire sauce
1 C. catsup

Mrs. William Byler

French Fried Chicken

Beat 2 eggs. Stir in ½ C. milk.
 Sift together and beat in:
1 C. flour
1 t. salt
1 t. baking powder
Add 1 t. melted fat.

 Dip chicken (which has been cooked) in mixture and fry in hot Crisco until golden brown.

Mrs. Eli D. Miller
Mrs. Henry D. Miller
Mrs. Eli A. Beachy

Baked Chicken

 Good for broilers. Dip each piece in melted butter. Roll in crushed corn flakes or Rice Krispies seasoned with salt and Lawry's seasoning salt. Place on cookie sheet and bake at 400° for 30 minutes on each side. Will get nice and crispy!

Lizzie Ann Erb

Barbecued Chicken

Brown chicken in hot fat. Brown 1 medium onion in 2 T. fat. Add:

2 T. vinegar
2 T. brown sugar
¼ C. lemon juice
1 C. catsup

3 T. Worcestershire sauce
½ T. mustard
1 C. water
½ C. chopped celery

 Simmer 30 minutes. Pour over chicken. Bake uncovered for 1 hour at 325°.

Mrs. Paul E. Miller

Canned Meatballs with Gravy

10 lbs. ground beef
4 C. oatmeal
4 C. milk
1 C. ketchup
3-4 eggs
chopped onion as desired

1/4 C. salt
pepper to taste
2 T. mustard
1/2 t. oregano
1/2 t. sage
2 t. seasoned salt

Mix thoroughly. Wet hands for easier handling to form into balls. Fry the meatballs, then make a thin brown gravy to pour over meatballs in jar. Cold pack 2 hours or 1 hour and 25 minutes at 10 lbs. pressure. A good way to stretch hamburger.

Mrs. Jonas Nisley

Baked Hamburgers

1 C. water
1/2 C. ketchup
2 T. mustard

2 T. vinegar
1/2 C. brown sugar
3/4 t. salt

Beat together with egg beater. Pour over hamburger patties and bake at 350° for 45 minutes. Note: This is also used to can hamburger patties.

Mrs. Eli D. Miller

Barbecued Beef Burgers

1 onion
1/2 C. catsup
2 T. brown sugar

2 T. vinegar
2 t. mustard
1 T. Worcestershire sauce

Heat together and pour over 1 qt. cut up beef chunks. Makes good sandwiches.

Mrs. J.L. Miller

Barbecued Chicken

2 T. flour
³/₄ C. water
2 T. vinegar
1 t. prepared mustard
1 T. brown sugar
2 t. Worcestershire sauce

2 C. canned tomatoes
1 T. chopped onion
1¹/₂ t. salt
¹/₂ t. pepper
¹/₂ t. garlic salt

Blend together and pour over browned chicken and bake at 350° for 1 hour.

Ada Burkholder

Barbecued Chicken

24 chicken halves/24 lbs. charcoal

Sauce for 24 Chicken Halves

10 oz. ReaLemon
4 oz. Worcestershire sauce
3 lbs. margarine (Blue Bonnet)

3 T. salt (if not salted before)
pepper

Spray on chicken while barbecuing.

Mrs. Albert M.L. Yoder

Oven Fried Chicken

Take 1 broiler or chicken. Roll in following mixture and fry. Then put in roaster and bake at 325° 35 minutes or until tender.

Mixture:
¹/₂ C. flour
2 t. salt

1¹/₂ t. paprika
¹/₄ t. pepper

Mary Schlabach

Sloppy Joes

1½ lb. hamburger
1½ t. salt
1 C. milk

¾ C. oatmeal
3 T. onions
pepper

Mix and let set. Brown then add sauce to mix.

Sauce

2 T. Worcestershire sauce
1 C. catsup

2 t. vinegar
½ C. water

Mrs. John A. Weaver

Sloppy Joes

Fry:
2½ lb. hamburger

1 medium onion

Drain and add:
2½ T. Worcestershire sauce
½ C. ketchup
1 can mushroom soup

⅓ C. brown sugar
1 T. mustard

Simmer 1 hour.

Mrs. Roman E. Raber

Ham Loaf

1 lb. ground ham
1 lb. ground veal
1 lb. hamburger
3 eggs
¼ t. pepper

1 t. salt
1 C. oatmeal
4 t. barbecue sauce
1 C. milk

Mix first 8 ingredients thoroughly. Add milk and mix well. Form loaf. Bake in slow oven at 325° for 1¾ hours.

Lizzie Raber

Ham Loaf

1½ C. milk
3 eggs
1 C. white crackers

1 C. graham crackers
2 lbs. hamburger
2 lbs. ham

Mix and bake at 325° for 1½ hour.

Mix ½ C. brown sugar, 1 t. mustard and 1 t. vinegar. Brush this sauce on top of ham loaf every half hour until done.

Canned Meat Loaf

15 lbs. hamburger
7 slices bread, crumbled
36 white cracker squares, crushed
1 C. oatmeal
3 C. water
pepper to taste
½ C. salt
4 eggs

Mix well. Pack in jars. Cold pack 4 hours. Can be eaten cold sliced from jar or heated.

Mary Ellen Troyer

Meat Loaf

1½ lbs. hamburger
¾ C. uncooked quick oats
1 egg, beaten
¾ C. milk

1½ t. salt
¼ C. onion
¼ t. pepper

Mix all ingredients and spread sauce over top and bake. Bake at 350° for 1 hour.

Sauce

⅓ C. catsup
1 T. mustard

2 T. brown sugar

Mrs. Levi H. Mast

Poor Man's Steak

2 lbs. hamburger
1 C. cracker crumbs
salt

pepper
milk (enough to hold
  together)

Shape in a roll. Put in refrigerator overnight. Slice and fry. Put in casserole and pour 1 can of cream of mushroom soup over all. Put in oven and bake at 325° for 1 hour.

Mrs. David E. Hershberger

Poor Man's Steak

3 lbs. hamburger
1 C. cracker crumbs
1 C. cold water

salt
pepper
1 can mushroom soup

Mix everything together except soup. Press on cookie sheet. Chill. Cut in squares, roll in flour and fry on both sides in a small amount of grease to golden brown but not too much. Place in baking dish. Don't dilute the soup. Spread soup over the meat. Put in oven and bake for 1 hour at 350°.

Mrs. Nelson A. Barkman
Mrs. Atlee J. Miller

Turkey Pot Pie

3 C. cut up turkey
1 C. peas
3 C. carrots, cut up
2 T. parsley
salt and pepper to taste

1/2 C. celery, cut up
3 potatoes, cut up
3 C. turkey broth or leftover
  gravy
1 onion, chopped

Cook vegetables in broth. Mix everything together and thicken like gravy. Make a pie crust and put in casserole. Then pour in the vegetable/turkey mixture and top with pie crust. Bake at 400° until crust is golden brown.

Mrs. Aden D. Troyer
Mrs. Fannie Yoder

Chicken Pudding

Put 3-4 C. deboned chicken (cooked) in bottom of buttered baking dish. Season to taste. Make batter of 2 beaten eggs, 2 C. flour and 3 t. melted butter and beat all together, adding a little milk if needed to make a thin batter. Pour over chicken and bake. Serve with gravy made from chicken broth.

Mrs. David Hershberger

Chicken-N-Stuff

6 C. bread cubes
¼ C. chopped celery
1 T. chopped onion
1 T. parsley flakes

¼ C. melted butter
2 eggs, beaten
salt and pepper to taste

Mix ingredients, then add enough hot water to moisten. Pour into a large casserole.

Topping

¼ C. butter
6 T. flour (rounded)
1 C. chicken broth

1 can cream of
   chicken soup
1 C. milk
2 C. cut up chicken, cooked

Melt butter, thicken with flour, salt and pepper. Add chicken broth, soup, milk and chicken and bring to boil. Pour over dressing and bake for 45 minutes at 350°.

Mrs. Emma Hershberger

Farmer's Delight

Press mixed hamburger in casserole dish and bake 1 hour. Put mashed potatoes on top of meat loaf. Add any gravy and top with Velveeta cheese. Put back in oven to melt cheese.

Mrs. Merlin Troyer

Meat Loaf

3 lb. hamburger
1½ C. cracker crumbs
2 C. tomato juice
½ C. onion

4 eggs, beaten
4 t. salt
½ t. pepper

Mix and press into pan. Bake at 350° for 1 hour.

Mrs. Roman E. Raber

Meat Loaf

1½ lbs. ground beef
¾ C. quick oatmeal
¼ C. chopped onion
¾ C. milk

1½ t. salt
¼ t. pepper
1 egg, beaten

Mix and press in a loaf pan. Put sauce on top. Bake 1 hour at 350°. Let set 5 minutes before serving.

Sauce

⅓ C. catsup
1 T. mustard

2 T. brown sugar

Taco Shells

1½ C. cold water
1 C. all-purpose flour
½ C. cornmeal

¼ t. salt
1 egg

Mix all together with hand beater and fry like pancakes. Pour scant ¼ C. dough in pan and rotate pan to make a nice round ring. We love it with tomatoes, hamburger (heated), cheddar cheese, lettuce and onions. Pour hot or mild taco sauce over all. Wrap up taco shell and eat.

Mrs. Dannie H. Burkholder

Meat Potato Quiche

Preheat oven to 425°. In 9" pie pan, stir together:

3 C. shredded raw potatoes
3 T. vegetable oil

Press evenly into pie crust shape. Bake for 15 minutes or until crust just begins to brown. Remove from oven. Layer on hot crust:

1 C. grated Swiss or cheddar cheese
1/4 C. onion (if desired)
3/4 C. cooked, diced chicken, ham or sausage

In a bowl beat together:

1 C. evaporated milk
2 eggs
1/2 t. salt
1/8 t. pepper

Pour egg mixture over other ingredients. Return to oven and bake 30 minutes or until lightly browned.

Mrs. John A. Miller

Barbecued Beef Sandwiches

1 C. onions, chopped   1/4 C. vegetable oil

Brown onions in oil then add:

1 C. water   2 T. vinegar
1 C. catsup   2 T. Worcestershire sauce
1 t. garlic salt   1 beef bouillon cube

Heat to boiling, then simmer 30 minutes. Add beef and simmer another 15-20 minutes.

Mary Esta Yoder

Meat for Sandwiches

1 C. ketchup
1/3 C. brown sugar
1/2 C. water

1/2 t. mustard
2 T. vinegar
1 1/2 lb. chipped ham

Mix ketchup, brown sugar, water, mustard and vinegar. Place ham in saucepan and top with sauce. Bake at 250° for 1 hour.

Mrs. John J. Troyer

Ground Beef Grand Style

1 pkg. Tater Tots
1 1/2 lb. ground beef, browned with onions
1/2 C. chopped onions
8 oz. pkg. cream cheese or Velveeta cheese
1 can mushroom or chicken soup
1/4 C. milk
1 t. salt
1/4 C. catsup

Mix everything together except cheese and Tater Tots. Put in pan. Put a layer of cheese over the hamburger then Tater Tots on top. Bake at 350° for 1 hour.

Erma Yoder

Barbecued Ham

12 lbs. chopped ham
10 t. vinegar
5 C. catsup

2 C. brown sugar
10 small onions

Mix catsup, vinegar, sugar and onions. Pour over chopped ham. Bake 1 hour in oven until hot. Can be heated on top of stove also. Serve on buns. Delicious sandwiches.

Mrs. Roy A. Miller

Ground Beef Grand Style

1 can oven ready biscuits
1 1/2 lb. ground beef
1/2 C. chopped onions
1 (8 oz.) pkg. cream cheese
1 can mushroom or chicken soup

1/2 C. milk
1 t. salt
1/4 C. catsup

Brown ground beef and onions. Add remaining ingredients and top with biscuits. Bake at 350° until biscuits are golden brown.

Mrs. Nelson A. Barkman

Meatball Casserole

1 lb. ground beef
1/2 lb. pork sausage
1/2 C. dry bread crumbs
1/3 C. evaporated milk

2 T. onions, chopped
1 t. chili powder
1/2 t. pepper

Combine and shape into meatballs. Brown and cover and heat 10 minutes on top of stove in a 2 qt. casserole. Uncover after it starts to cook.

1 can mushroom soup
1 can cream of celery soup

1 C. evaporated milk
1/2 C. water

Combine and heat until steaming. Pour over meatballs and top with biscuits. Bake at 400° for 20-25 minutes.

Cheese Joes

2 1/2 lb. hamburger
1 t. salt
  Fry together and add:

1/4 t. pepper
1/4 C. chopped onion

1 C. water
1/2 C. catsup
  Cook 1 minute. Let set 5 minutes then add:

1 C. quick oats

1 can mushroom soup

1 can celery soup

Put on buns while hot with a slice of cheese.

Mary Esta Yoder

Barbecued Beef Sandwiches

1 onion
3/4 C. catsup
2 T. brown sugar
2 T. vinegar

2 t. mustard
2 t. white sauce
1 t. salt
1 qt. beef chunks

Mix together and pour over beef chunks.

Mrs. Henry E. Mast

Deluxe Carrot Casserole

12 medium carrots (approx. 6 C.)

Slice and cook until tender. Do not overcook. Drain. In medium saucepan sauté one small minced onion in 1/4 C. oleo. Add 1/4 C. flour, 1 t. salt, 1/4 t. dry mustard, 1/8 t. black pepper and 1/4 t. celery salt. Stir in 2 C. milk and 1/2 lb. Velveeta cheese. Stir constantly as cheese melts. Pour cheese sauce over carrots in a greased casserole. Top with 1 1/2 C. crushed potato chips. Bake at 350° for 25 minutes.

Mary Esta Yoder

Wigglers

2 lbs. hamburger
5 slices bacon
1 1/2 C. celery
1 can mushroom soup
1 pkg. spaghetti
1 qt. tomato soup

2 onions
2 C. potatoes
1 1/2 C. carrots
1 qt. peas
3/4 lb. cheese

Fry bacon. Fry hamburger and onions in bacon grease. Put in bottom of roaster. Add cooked potatoes, carrots, celery and peas and add mushroom soup. Cook spaghetti, add bacon and cheese, pour tomato soup over top and bake 1 hour.

Mrs. Henry E. Mast

Baked Beans

2 C. small or medium dried beans (soak overnight)
2 t. salt
1/8 t. pepper
1/2 C. brown sugar
1/2 C. minced onions
3 T. good brown bacon drippings
1 t. mustard
4 C. tomato juice
ham, bacon or hot dogs (optional)

Cook beans till soft then add the rest of ingredients and cook uncovered for 1 hour.

Mrs. David R. Yoder

Baked Beans

1 can red kidney beans (dark)
1 can butter or lima beans
28 oz. can pork-n-beans

Mix together. Don't drain juice off. In skillet fry 1/2 lb. bacon, cut in strips. Start cooking bacon but don't brown. Leave some grease in pan and add:

2 small onions, chopped   1 C. ketchup
1 C. brown sugar   1 t. prepared mustard

Heat mixture and pour over beans and mix well. Bake at 350° for at least 1 hour with no lid or longer than 1 hour if desired. Very good.

Mrs. Dannie H. Burkholder   Mrs. Henry D. Miller
Mrs. Nelson A. Barkman   Mrs. John J. Troyer
                                        Mrs. Andy A. Yoder

Pork and Beans

8 lbs. navy beans
1/3 C. salt
4 qt. tomato juice
1/2 t. pepper
1 t. cinnamon
1 large onion

1 1/2 lb. bacon or hot dogs
9 C. white sugar
4 C. brown sugar
1 t. mustard
26 oz. bottle ketchup
4 T. cornstarch

Soak beans overnight. Cook beans till soft. Mix the rest of ingredients together and cook a few minutes. Then add to the beans and mix well. Put in jars and seal. Makes around 15 qt. Cold pack 1/2 hour.

Mrs. Dan Erb
Mrs. Emanuel H. Yoder

Delicious Barbecued Beans

2 qt. baby lima beans, cooked
2 qt. soup beans, cooked
2 qt. red kidney beans, cooked
2 qt. pea beans, cooked
1 qt. chopped sweet pickles
1 stalk celery, cut up fine
6 large onions, chopped
1 bottle barbecue sauce
tomatoes as needed
brown sugar and white sugar to suit taste
salt
1/4 C. vinegar
1 C. clear Karo
2 C. flour to thicken
   Mix everything together. Put in jars and cold pack 2 hours.

Mrs. Eli A. Beachy

Egg Omelet Dish

6 eggs, beaten
2 C. milk
2 C. bread crumbs

1 C. shredded Velveeta
1 lb. bulk sausage, browned
and chilled

Mix and let set overnight. Bake at 350° till set and light brown. Delicious!

Mrs. J.L. Miller

Breakfast Sausage Casserole

6 eggs
2 C. milk
6 slices bread, cubed

1 t. salt
4 oz. mild cheese, cubed
1 lb. sausage

Refrigerate overnight and bake at 350° for 45 minutes.

Lizzie Raber

Breakfast Casserole

Beat 6 eggs, add ham, sausage or bacon, onion, salt and pepper, 2 C. milk and 6 pieces bread. Pour into greased cake pan. Refrigerate overnight. Bake at 350° for ½ hour. Cheese can be put on top if desired.

Mary Ellen Troyer

Egg Supper Dish

3 T. butter
½ t. dry mustard
¼ t. celery salt
1 C. crushed potato chips

2 T. flour
1½ C. milk
⅛ t. pepper
6 hard-boiled eggs, sliced

Melt butter, add dry ingredients and last add milk. Pour over eggs and chips in layers in dish. Bake in oven at 350° till heated through.

Mrs. Atlee J. Miller

Egg Dutch

5 T. flour
2½ C. milk
8 eggs

salt
½ t. baking powder

Blend together. Put butter in skillet and fry slowly.

Mrs. Adam Yoder

Potato Puffs

1 C. mashed potatoes (leftover)
1-2 eggs, beaten
¼ t. salt

¼-½ C. flour
1 t. baking powder

Mix well and drop by teaspoon in deep lard or Mazola oil. Fry until brown on both sides.

Mary Schlabach
Mrs. Abe E. Mast

Potato and Egg Dish

Slice 3 good size potatoes. Cook. Boil 3 eggs. Make a white sauce of 3 T. butter in which you fry 2 small onions, add 2 T. flour and ½ t. salt and pepper. When light brown add 3 C. milk and bring to a boil. Put in casserole layer by layer of potatoes, eggs, then sauce and cover with bread crumbs and bake at 350° till brown.

Mrs. J.L. Miller

Hush Puppies

3 C. yellow cornmeal
1 C. flour
3 T. baking powder
3 T. sugar

3½ t. salt
3 eggs
2½ C. milk

Mix all ingredients and drop by teaspoon into hot fat. Cook till brown (cook as you would for french fries).

Mrs. Clara Mast

Easy Homemade Pizza

Crust:

4 C. flour	1⅓ C. milk
6 t. baking powder	⅔ C. shortening
2 t. salt	

Combine milk and shortening with the rest of the ingredients.

Pizza Sauce

6 oz. can tomato paste or catsup	1 t. oregano
6 oz. can tomato juice	⅛ t. hot pepper
1 t. garlic	¼ t. cloves
2 t. sugar	1 small onion

Put hamburger on dough rolled out on pizza pan. Add pizza sauce and Velveeta cheese.

Mrs. Emanuel J. Miller

Jiffy Pizza Dough

2 C. flour	⅔ C. milk
1 T. baking powder	⅓ C. salad oil
1 t. salt	

Mix together. Press in pan.

Mrs. Henry D. Miller

Pizza Crust

1 C. warm water	2 T. oil
1 T. yeast	2½ C. flour
2 T. sugar	1 t. salt

Mix together and let set for 5 minutes. Press into pan. Makes 1 pizza.

Mrs. John A. Weaver

Potluck Potatoes

2 lbs. potatoes
½ C. butter
1 can cream of mushroom,
   chicken or celery soup
1 t. onion salt

¼ t. pepper
1 pt. sour cream
2 C. Velveeta cheese
1 t. Lawry's seasoning salt

Slice potatoes, cook till almost tender. Combine the rest of the ingredients and heat till cheese is melted. Put in layers in casserole and cover with 2 C. crushed corn flake crumbs. Mix with ½ C. melted butter. Bake at 350° for 45 minutes.

Mrs. J.L. Miller
Mrs. Emanuel H. Yoder
Mrs. David Beachy

Chicken Casserole

9 slices bread
1 can canned mushroom pieces
2 C. milk (or part chicken broth)
9 slices Velveeta cheese
¼ C. butter

4 C. cooked chicken, cut up
½ C. salad dressing
4 eggs
2 cans celery soup

Grease the roaster with the butter. Break bread in bottom of casserole. Put chicken and mushroom pieces on top. Beat eggs, milk and salad dressing and pour on top of bread and chicken. Cover with cheese and put celery soup on top and refrigerate overnight. Bake at 350° for 1½ hours. Stir it a little every so often so the liquid goes down to the bread and is absorbed. This expands when baking so be sure to use a big enough roaster.

Mrs. Aden D. Troyer

Hash Brown Potato Casserole

2 lb. potatoes, cooked
1/2 C. melted butter
10 oz. or 2 C. cheddar cheese
1/4 t. pepper
1/2 C. onion, chopped
1 pt. sour cream

1 can cream of
   chicken soup
1 t. salt
2 C. crushed corn flakes
1/4 C. melted butter

Put potatoes in a large mixing bowl with 1/2 C. melted butter and add salt, pepper, onions, soup, sour cream and cheese. Blend thoroughly. Pour into greased 9" x 13" casserole and top with crushed corn flakes mixed with 1/4 C. melted butter. Bake at 350° for 45 minutes.

Mrs. Clara Mast

Shipwreck Casserole

1 1/2 lb. hamburger, fried with onions to your taste. Add salt.
1 qt. cubed potatoes
1 pt. carrots
1 pt. peas

1 can cream of mushroom
   soup
1 can cream of chicken soup

Add salt to each vegetable, cooking each vegetable till soft. Put some cut up celery in. Layer in a casserole and add cream of chicken soup and cream of mushroom soup. Add enough milk to make it thin. Bake at 350° until heated all through then put Velveeta cheese on top. One meal dish with applesauce and fruit. It's good.

Mrs. Abe J. Schlabach

"Never mistake knowledge for wisdom.
One helps you make a living;
the other helps you make a life."

Pizza Casserole

1-2 lbs. hamburger
$\frac{1}{2}$ green pepper
1 can mushroom soup
1 pt. pizza sauce
1 can mushrooms (not drained)

$\frac{1}{4}$ t. garlic powder
$\frac{1}{4}$ t. oregano
$\frac{1}{4}$ C. Parmesan cheese
8 oz. wide noodles

Brown hamburger. Add salt, pepper and onion to taste. Cook noodles 3-5 minutes. Drain. Place in bottom of baking dish. Add hamburger mixture and remaining ingredients. Top with mozzaralla cheese and pepperoni. Bake at 350° for $\frac{1}{2}$ hour.

Mary Ellen Troyer
Mrs. Henry D. Miller

Mrs. David E. Hershberger
Mrs. Paul Frey
Mrs. Dennis B. Miller

Mock Turkey

2 lb. hamburger, browned in butter
2 cans cream of chicken soup
1 can cream of celery soup
4 C. milk
1 loaf of bread, toasted
salt and pepper to taste

Mix together and place in casserole. Bake at 350° for 45 minutes.

Mrs. Aden J. Hershberger
Mrs. Marlin Yoder

Mock Turkey

Toast 1 loaf bread
Fry 2 lbs. hamburger (but not brown) with 1 onion. Add 2 cans cream of chicken soup, 1 can celery soup and salt. I add some potatoes. Mix well. Put in oven and bake at 300° for 1 hour.

Mrs. Henry D. Miller

Chicken Casserole

3 chickens, cooked and deboned
27 slices bread, diced

Put chicken and bread in layers.

6 eggs
3 C. chicken broth
3/4 C. milk
3/4 C. salad dressing

Beat and pour over chicken and bread. Top with 3 cans cream of celery soup and 1 can mushroom soup. Top with Velveeta cheese. Bake at 350° for about 1 3/4 hour.

Mrs. David J.C. Yoder

Sausage-Egg Casserole

6 eggs
1 1/2 C. milk
3 slices diced white bread
1 t. dry mustard

1 t. salt
1 lb. ground sausage
1 C. grated cheese

Brown sausage well and drain thoroughly. Beat eggs, milk, mustard and salt together. Add bread, cheese and sausage. Refrigerate overnight. Bake at 350° for 50 minutes or until done. Serves 8.

Mrs. Lloyd Miller
Lizzie Ann Erb

Hamburger Casserole

1/2 lb. hamburger, fried with 1/2 C. onion. Add:

8 oz. cream cheese
1/4 C. ketchup
1/4 C. milk

1 can mushroom soup
pinch of salt

Bake at 350° for 10 minutes. Put one can of biscuits on top and bake until biscuits are brown.

Lizzie Ann Erb

Chicken Gumbo

9 slices bread
4 C. cut up chicken
1/4 C. melted butter
1/2 C. salad dressing
4 eggs, beaten
1 C. milk

1 C. chicken broth
salt to taste
9 slices Velveeta cheese
2 cans cream of celery soup
buttered bread crumbs

Butter bottom of medium roaster. Put 9 slices bread in bottom. Add cut up cooked chicken. Mix butter, salad dressing, beaten eggs, milk, broth and salt and pour over bread and chicken. Top with Velveeta cheese and celery soup and cover with buttered crumbs. Bake at 350° for 1 1/4 hours. Cover with foil. Take foil off last 15 mintues to crisp bread. May be made and refrigerated the day before.

Alma E. Stutzman
Mary Schlabach
Mrs. Junior A. Yoder

Rice Casserole

1 lb. hamburger
1 can mushroom or chicken soup
pepper or other seasoning
1/2 C. celery
1/2 C. potatoes, cut up
salt to taste

1/2 C. rice
2 C. water
1 onion, cut up
1/2 C. carrots
1 can tomato paste
1 pepper, cut up optional

In skillet brown hamburger and onions. Add tomato paste or juice. Add rice, water, soup, peppers, potatoes, carrots and celery. Season to suit your taste. If you like you can add a can of peas, paprika or chili powder. Pour in casserole and bake at 350° for 1 1/2 hours. Stir several times. This may be used with chicken instead of hamburger and cheddar cheese soup instead of water.

Mrs. Alfred D. Stutzman

Chicken Rice Casserole

2 C. rice, cooked in 2½ C. chicken broth (cook 20 minutes covered, low heat)
2 C. celery, sauted lightly in oleo
2 C. undiluted mushroom soup
1½ C. real mayonnaise
2 T. chopped onion
2 C. chopped chicken, deboned

Mix gently and put in greased casserole. Mix crushed cornflakes and melted oleo and put on top. Bake at 350° for 45 minutes.

Mrs. David D. Miller

Chicken Pie

Crust:
2 C. flour
½ C. milk
2 T. lard

1½ t. baking powder
salt to taste

Melt 1 T. butter and mix with 3 T. flour. Cook until creamy.
Add:
1 qt. chicken broth
1 C. cooked potatoes
1½ C. cooked carrots

1 C. cooked chicken
1 C. cooked celery

Cover top with dough crust. Bake at 350°.

Mrs. David E. Hershberger

Penny Saver Casserole

6 hot dogs, thinly sliced
1 C. peas
2 T. minced onion
1 can cream of mushroom soup

4 medium potatoes,
  cooked and diced
1 t. mustard
½ C. butter

Combine potatoes, onions and butter in casserole. Add peas, soup and mustard to the first mixture. Dot with sliced hot dogs (pennies). Cover and bake at 350° for 25 minutes.

Mrs. Henry D. Miller

Pepper and Hamburger Casserole

Cook 4 C. cubed potatoes, ½ C. rice and cut up peppers (as many as you wish). Cook till soft. Fry 2 lb. hamburger in skillet till brown. Mix all together and make a sauce with tomato juice (1 pt.), ketchup, Tabasco sauce, salt and sugar to taste. Thicken and put in casserole. Bake at 350° for 30 minutes.

Edna Troyer

One Step Macaroni & Cheese

4 C. uncooked elbow macaroni
6 C. milk
2 t. Worcestershire sauce

1 t. salt
2 C. Velveeta or less
paprika

Combine ingredients. Put in casserole. Bake at 350° for 50 minutes. Cover with tinfoil.

Edna Troyer

Turkey or Chicken Supreme

2 C. cooked chicken
2 C. uncooked macaroni
2 cans cream of chicken soup
2 C. milk
1 C. grated cheese

½ C. chopped onion
½ t. salt
¼ t. pepper
3 T. butter

Combine all ingredients and put in greased casserole. Refrigerate overnight. Bake at 350° for 1½ hours.

Mrs. Levi Beachy
Mary Esta Yoder

Skillet Macaroni & Beef

1½ lbs. ground beef
1 t. salt
¼ t. pepper
½ C. diced onion
2 (8 oz.) cans Hunt's tomato sauce or use your own canned tomato juice

1½ t. Worcestershire
  sauce
1 C. water
2 C. uncooked macaroni

Brown beef and remove meat from skillet and cook macaroni and onions in beef fat till they are covered with fat. Put beef in macaroni again and add other ingredients. Add a little sugar to taste. Cover and simmer till macaronis are done.

Mrs. Paul A. Yoder

Casserole

1 qt. potatoes, diced
1 qt. carrots, diced
1½ lb. hamburger fried (add salt and pepper)
1 onion
1 can cream of mushroom soup
1 can cream of chicken soup
1" slice Velveeta cheese on top

Combine ingredients and bake at 350° until vegetables are tender.

Mrs. John J. Troyer

"Anything Goes" Casserole

Place bread slices into a buttered 8" x 8" pan. Top with cheese slices then put in sausage, ham, tuna or any kind of meat. Top with bread slices. Pour mixture of 4 eggs, 1½ C. milk, salt and pepper on top. Cover and refrigerate overnight or at least 8 hours. Bake uncovered at 350° for 1 hour or till brown. We like 1 pt. canned hamburger chopped with some catsup to suit your taste. Adding oregano makes it taste more like pizza.

Mrs. Levi Beachy

Pot Pie to Bake

2 C. flour
1/2 C. cream
pinch of salt

1/4 C. butter
2 t. baking powder

Mix this like pie dough. Add more cream if you need to. Roll out and cut in small 1 1/2" squares and bake on a cookie sheet. Make any fruit pie filling (don't make it as thick as pie filling). Put the baked squares in a dish and pour filling over them and serve right away with milk and sugar. A good supper.

Mrs. Abe J. Schlabach

Casserole

1 stick oleo or butter, browned
1 C. rice
1 can Campbell's lite onion soup

1 can beef consommé
2 oz. can mushrooms

Brown butter. Add rice and pour into 1 1/2 qt. casserole. Add soups and mushrooms. Bake at 375° for 45 minutes covered and 15 minutes uncovered.

Mary Ellen Troyer

El Paso Casserole

1 3/4 lb. Velveeta cheese
2 lb. chipped ham
1 1/2 lb. noodles, cooked

White Sauce

1/2 lb. butter
1 C. flour

1/2 gal. milk
1 can celery soup

Cook noodles in salt water. Blend cheese and ham in white sauce. Pour over noodles in oiled pan. Sprinkle with toasted bread crumbs. Bake at 350° for 25 minutes.

Lizzie Raber

Escalloped Carrots

12 carrots or more, cooked
1/4 C. flour
1/4 t. dry mustard
3 C. buttered bread crumbs
1 t. salt
1/4 t. celery salt

1/4 C. oleo or butter
1 onion, diced
2 C. milk
1/2 lb. Velveeta cheese
1/8 t. pepper

Do not overcook carrots. Cook onions in butter for 2-3 minutes. Make a white sauce with flour and milk. Add mustard, salt, celery salt and pepper. Add cheese. Put carrots in a 2 qt. casserole. Pour white sauce over carrots. Top with buttered bread crumbs. You may want to use other vegetables such as cauliflower or broccoli. Bake at 350° for 30 minutes.

Mrs. Merlin Troyer

Marinated Carrots

5 C. carrots, sliced
1 small green pepper
1/2 C. salad oil
1/2 C. sugar
1/4 C. vinegar

1 t. salt
1 medium onion, sliced
1 can tomato soup
1 t. prepared mustard
1/2 t. pepper

Cook carrots and peppers till tender. Drain and cool. Mix together tomato soup, oil, sugar, vinegar, mustard, salt and pepper. Pour over carrots, onion and pepper slices. Refrigerate for 24 hours or overnight. Drain and serve cold.

Mrs. Aden J. Raber

Onion Patties

3/4 C. flour
1 t. salt
2 t. baking powder
1 T. cornmeal

1 T. sugar
2/3 C. milk
2 1/3 C. chopped onions

Mix together and form patties. Deep fry.

Mary Schlabach

Ham & Potato Scallop

1 can cream of mushroom soup
1/4 C. milk
5 C. sliced potatoes

1/2 C. chopped onion
1 T. butter
2 C. cooked or canned ham

Cut ham in 1/2" cubes. Blend soup and milk, add potatoes, diced ham and onion. Mix. Put in greased 2 qt. casserole. Dot top with butter. Bake uncovered in moderate oven at 350° for 1 hour. Cover and continue baking 45 minutes or until potatoes are done. Trim top with parsley. Makes 6 servings. Add a little Velveeta cheese before it's done.

Mrs. Roy A. Schlabach

French Fried Onion Rings

1 C. pancake mix
1 egg
1 T. Wesson oil
1 bouillon cube or
　1/2 t. chicken soup base

1/2 C. boiling water
1" oil at 350°
peeled and sliced onions

Dissolve bouillon cube or soup base in boiling water and cool. Beat together pancake mix, egg and oil. Add cooled water mixture. Dip onion rings in the liquid mixture, drain a minute and fry them in the heated oil.

Anna Kay Bowman
Mrs. Nelson A. Barkman

Ham and Potatoes

3 gal. potatoes, cooked with jackets and peeled and sliced. Add:

3 cans cream of mushroom soup
3 cans cream of celery soup
1 can cheddar cheese soup
1 can evaporated milk or cream
5 lbs. chopped ham, cooked

Add sweet milk so it won't be so thick. Mix and bake in roaster at 350° for 1 hour.

Mrs. Roy J. Wengerd

Shipwreck

1 1/2 lb. hamburger, browned
onions, sliced or diced
1 qt. potatoes, cooked and diced
1 pt. carrots, cooked and diced
8 oz. pkg. noodles, cooked
1 pt. peas
1 can cream of chicken soup
1 can cream of celery soup
1 can mushroom soup

Place in order given in casserole and bake at 350° for 1 hour.

Ada Burkholder

Bar-B-Q Ham

12 lbs. chipped ham
10 T. vinegar
10 small onions, chopped

5 C. catsup
2 C. brown sugar

Mix catsup, sugar, vinegar and onions. Pour on chipped ham. Bake 1 hour in oven until hot. Could be heated on top of stove also. Serve on buns. Makes a big batch.

Mrs. Emanuel Weaver

Corn Balls and Dressing

Brown 1 C. celery and 1/2 C. onion in 1/2 C. butter. Add 1 pt. cream style corn, salt and pepper to taste, 1 1/2 t. poultry seasoning or sage and 1 C. water. Bring to boil and pour this over 1 (16 oz.) loaf white bread. Add 3 beaten egg yolks. Toss thoroughly. Make into balls and put in greased loaf pan. Melt 1/2 C. butter and pour over the balls. Bake 25 minutes at 375°. Serve with creamed chicken.

Mrs. David D. Miller

Chicken Strata

8 slices bread, cubed
1/2 C. onion, chopped
1/2 C. salad dressing
dash of pepper
1 1/2 C. milk
1/2 C. cheese, grated

2 C. cooked chicken
(bite size pieces)
1/2 C. celery
3/4 t. salt
2 eggs, beaten
1 can mushroom soup

Place half of bread cubes in baking dish. Combine chicken, vegetables, salad dressing and seasonings. Spread over bread. Add remaining bread. Combine eggs and milk and pour over bread cubes. Cover. Refrigerate 1 hour or overnight. Add soup, bake at 350° for 50 minutes. Add cheese and bake till melted.

Mrs. Roy A. Schlabach

Quick and Easy Sandwiches

1 1/2 lb. hamburger
1 small box Velveeta cheese
1 small onion
1 can cream of mushroom soup

Brown hamburger and onion till brown. Add soup and cheese. Stir till melted. Serve on buns.

Mrs. Daniel Barkman

Pickled Carrots

2 lb. carrots cooked (not too soft)
1 green pepper, chopped
1 onion, sliced
1 can tomato soup
3/4 C. vinegar

1/2 t. prepared mustard
1 t. Worcestershire sauce
3/4 C. white sugar
1/2 C. Wesson oil

Combine last 6 ingredients and heat and pour over carrots, pepper and onion. Refrigerate overnight.

Lizzie Raber

Corn Ball Bake

1 C. celery, chopped
$^{1}/_{2}$ C. onions, chopped

Brown in $^{1}/_{2}$ C. butter. Add:

1 can cream style corn (2$^{1}/_{2}$ C.)
$^{1}/_{2}$ t. salt
$^{1}/_{4}$ t. pepper
1$^{1}/_{2}$ t. poultry seasoning or sage
1 C. water

Bring to boil and pour over slices of a 16 oz. loaf of bread. Add 3 beaten egg yolks and toss thoroughly. Let cool; form balls and put in a buttered 9" x 13" dish. Melt $^{1}/_{2}$ C. butter and pour some on each ball. Bake at 375° for 25 minutes. This is good served with creamed chicken.

Mrs. Edwin M. Troyer

*"All of us could take a lesson from the weather.
It pays no attention to criticism."*

*"Character is what you know you are,
not what others think you are."*

- Notes -

Soups

Bean with Bacon Soup to Can

4 lb. navy beans (soak overnight)
12 qt. water
2 lb. bacon
2 C. chopped onion
8 C. mashed potatoes

4 C. diced celery
4 C. diced carrots
2 qt. to 1 pt. tomato juice
16 t. salt
2 t. pepper

Cook navy beans till soft. Cook vegetables till soft. Put carrots and celery through Victorio strainer. Put drippings from bacon in soup. Pressure cooker 60 minutes at 10 lbs. pressure. Makes 14 qt.

Ada Mae Raber

Bean with Bacon Soup

2 lb. dried navy beans (soak overnight)
3 C. chopped onions
2 C. diced celery
2½ C. tomato juice
2 bay leaves

2 lb. bacon
2 C. diced potatoes
2 C. sliced carrots
1 t. pepper

Cook navy beans till soft. Cook together onions, potatoes, celery and carrots till soft. Fry bacon and crumble in small pieces. Add bacon drippings, simmer for awhile then cold pack for 3 hours or pressure can for 75 minutes at 10 lb. pressure.

Mrs. Uriah W. Hostetler

Chili Soup

Brown together:
5 lbs. hamburger
3 C. onions, chopped
  Add:
2 qt. tomato juice
2 qt. water
2 C. ketchup

2 T. salt
1 T. pepper

½ gal. kidney beans
1½ t. chili powder
1 T. salt

Cook well. Put in jars and cold pack 2 hours. Makes 2 gallons.

Mrs. Emanuel H. Yoder

Chili Soup

5 lbs. hamburger, fried with 2 onions, cut up, and 2 sticks oleo. Add:
6 qt. tomato juice
1 bottle catsup
4 C. cooked kidney beans
1 t. pepper
3 T. salt
2½ C. brown sugar
1 t. chili powder if you desire

Mix together and cold pack 1½ hours.

Mrs. David D. Miller

Broccoli Soup

Simmer 1 small can chicken broth and 2 bouillon cubes and 10 oz. frozen chopped broccoli till tender but still crunchy. Use as much broccoli as desired. Simmer in large pan till tender: 3 chopped onions and 3 T. oleo. Add 4 T. flour, ½ t. salt and pepper. Stir until thick. Add and stir in 2¼ C. milk and 1 C. American cheese, grated. Stir till cheese melts. Now add chicken broth and broccoli to this mixture and add 1 C. leftover mashed potatoes. The more mashed potatoes you add the thicker the soup and the better it gets in taste. Delicious!

Lizzie Raber

Vegetable Soup

1 qt. carrots, cooked	1 qt. onions, soaked
1 qt. potatoes, cooked	½ C. white sugar
1 qt. soup beans, cooked	1 T. chili powder
1 qt. peas, cooked	2 lb. hamburger, fried
1 qt. corn, cooked	7 qt. tomato juice
1 C. spaghetti, cooked	salt and pepper to taste
1 qt. celery, soaked	

Cook vegetables separately then mix together and put in jars, seal and cold pack 3 hours.

Mrs. Henry M. Troyer

- Notes -

Cereal, Etc.

Breakfast Cereal

10 C. rolled oats
4 C. wheat flour
2 C. brown sugar
1 C. coconut
3 C. graham cracker pieces

1 C. vegetable oil
1 C. maple syrup
1 C. raisins
1³/₄ C. chocolate chips

Mix everything except raisins and chocolate chips. Bake in oven at 375° till nice and brown (30-45 minutes), stirring often. Add raisins and chocolate chips after baking but while still warm.

Mrs. Elmer Yoder

Cereal

1¹/₂ C. brown sugar
8 C. oatmeal
4 C. whole wheat flour
2 t. salt

3 t. soda
2¹/₂ C. butter, melted
4 C. coconut
2 pkg. graham crackers

Crush graham crackers. Mix all together. Bake at 250° for 45 minutes. When finished add 1 lb. chocolate chips and 1 lb. butterscotch chips immediately. Stir often. We eat this on top of other cereal, like corn flakes.

Mary Schlabach

Breakfast Cereal

2 C. rolled oats
2 C. wheat flour
1 C. brown sugar
1 t. soda

1 t. salt
¹/₂ C. butter
¹/₂ C. coconut

Mix until crumbly like pie dough, then put on cookie sheet and toast in oven at 400° for 20 minutes. Stir a few times while in oven.

Mrs. Nelson A. Barkman

Apple Crisp

1 C. flour
³/₄ C. oatmeal
1 t. cinnamon

¹/₂ C. shortening
1 C. brown sugar

Mix ingredients together until crumbly. Press only half of mixture in pan. Put 5 c. diced apples over crumbs. Combine:

1 C. brown sugar
1¹/₂ C. water

2 t. cornstarch
1 t. vanilla

Cook mixture until thick and clear. Pour over apples and top with remaining crumbs and bake at 350°.

Lizzie Raber

Cornmeal Mush

4 C. water
1 t. salt

1 C. cornmeal

Put water on to boil, saving at least a cup to stir with cornmeal. Pour mixture into boiling water, stirring constantly until it boils thoroughly. Turn burner to low heat, cover kettle, stir occasionally. Cook for an hour or more. Eat hot with butter and syrup or milk. Or pour in dish to cool, slice and fry.

Apple Dumplings

Dough

2 C. flour
¹/₂ C. shortening
1 t. salt

²/₃ C. milk
¹/₂ C. sugar
2 t. baking powder

Sprinkle on apples before baking:

2 T. butter
¹/₄ t. cinnamon

Mix together dough ingredients and knead like pie dough. Roll out and cut squares to fit apple halves. Wrap dough around apples and bake at 350° for 45 minutes or until golden brown. Serve.

Mrs. Henry E. Mast

Rolled Oats Pone

½ C. sour milk
½ C. brown sugar
½ t. soda
pinch of salt
½ t. vanilla

1 C. flour
½ C. quick oats
1½ T. vegetable oil
1 egg

Mix and bake at 350°. Makes 1 pie pan full. Serve with milk and strawberries.

Mary Schlabach

Rolled Oats Pone

1 C. rolled oats
1 C. milk
  Soak 1 hour. Add:
1½ C. sugar
2 C. flour
2 eggs

1 t. soda
½ t. salt

Mix and bake at 350°. Serve with fruit and milk.

Corn Pone

1 egg
½ C. sugar
¼ C. shortening
½ C. sour milk

½ t. soda
½ t. baking powder
¾ C. cornmeal

Mix and sprinkle with sugar before baking. Serve with your favorite fruit and milk.

Mary Esta Yoder

Grape Nuts Cereal

5 lbs. brown sugar
8 lbs. whole wheat flour
1¼ T. salt
¾ lb. melted oleo

1½ t. maple flavoring
2 T. vanilla
2½ qt. buttermilk
3 T. soda

Put dry ingredients except soda in a large bowl. Dissolve soda in buttermilk before adding to dry ingredients. Last add oleo and flavoring. Mix well. The dough should be fairly thick. Bake in loaf pans at 350° until done. Cool. Crumble and toast until golden brown.

Mrs. Jonas J. Miller

Waffles or Pancakes

2 C. sifted all-purpose flour
3 T. sugar
1 t. salt
3 t. baking powder

2 eggs, separated
1¾ C. milk
4 T. melted butter

Sift dry ingredients together in mixing bowl. Add egg yolks and milk, slowly beating it till batter is smooth. Then add melted butter and stiffly beaten egg whites.

Mary Schlabach

Extra Special Apple Crisp

6 C. sliced apples
1 C. sugar
1 C. water
2 T. cornstarch

1 C. flour
¾ C. quick oatmeal
1 C. brown sugar
½ C. melted butter

Spread apples in 9" square baking dish. Cook sugar, water and cornstarch until clear and thickened. Pour over apples, sprinkle with cinnamon. Mix the flour, oatmeal, sugar and butter until crumbly. Sprinkle over apples. Bake at 350° for 40 minutes or until apples are tender.

Mrs. Paul A. Yoder

- Notes -

Candy

Fudge Candy

3 C. white sugar
3/4 C. butter
2/3 C. evaporated milk
12 oz. chocolate chips

1 jar marshmallow creme
1 C. nuts
1 t. vanilla

Combine sugar, butter and milk. Bring to a boil. Stir 5 minutes over medium heat to soft ball stage (238°). Remove from heat and stir in chips. Add marshmallow creme, nuts and vanilla. Beat until well blended. Pour into a greased pan and cut in squares.

Mattie Hershberger

Caramels

1 lb. brown sugar
1 can Eagle Brand milk
1/2 lb. butter

1 C. white corn syrup
pinch of salt

Mix and boil until firm ball stage, stirring often. Remove from heat, add 1 t. vanilla and beat till firm. Pour into pan and let cool. Cut in pieces and wrap in wax paper.

Mrs. Henry D. Miller

Chocolate Covered Cherries

10 oz. maraschino cherries
1/8 lb. soft butter

1/4 C. cherry juice
1 lb. powdered sugar

Mix sugar, juice and butter thoroughly. Make small balls, press dough with thumb to make a dent to put cherry in. Fold dough over it, roll into ball again. Dip within 2 hours or centers will get soft and hard to dip. Spread cherries on towels overnight for easy work. Cherries can be cut in half and only a half used in each ball.

Mrs. Nelson A. Barkman

218

Rice Krispie Treat

¹/₄ C. melted oleo
4 C. miniature marshmallows
5 C. Rice Krispies

Melt oleo in large saucepan. Add marshmallows, stirring until completely melted. Cook 2 minutes longer. Pour over Rice Krispies. Press in buttered cookie sheet. Cut in squares when cool.

Mary Schlabach

Never Fail Fudge

¹/₃ C. butter
4¹/₂ C. sugar
14¹/₂ oz. can evaporated milk
1 C. marshmallow creme
2 t. vanilla

1 bar (13oz.) sweet
   chocolate, grated
12 oz. semisweet
   chocolate chips
2 C. walnuts, chopped

Combine butter, sugar and milk and boil 5¹/₂ minutes. Remove from heat and add remaining ingredients except nuts. Beat until well mixed and add nuts. Spoon into buttered pan. Cool until firm then cut. This makes 5 lbs.

Miss Verna L. Miller

Puffed Rice Candy

2 C. brown sugar
¹/₂ C. maple flavored Karo

¹/₄ C. water
1 t. vinegar

Cook 10 minutes then put in 2 t. butter and cook to a hard boil. Pour over 1 pkg. puffed rice.

Katie B. Yoder

219

Special K Bars

1 C. sugar
1 C. peanut butter

1 C. light Karo
6 C. Special K cereal

Mix sugar and Karo and boil 30 seconds. Add peanut butter and beat until smooth. Pour over cereal and place in buttered baking dish. Melt chocolate and spread over candy.

Mrs. Albert A. Raber, Jr.

Hopscotch Candy

Combine in top of double boiler:

1/2 C. peanut butter

1 C. butterscotch chips

Place over hot, not boiling, water and stir until blended. Add and stir until well coated: 1 can (2 C.) chow mein noodles, 2 C. miniature marshmallows. Drop by teaspoon onto wax paper lined cookie sheet. Chill.

Mrs. Nelson A. Barkman

Caramel Corn
Fit for a King

Pop enough popcorn to fill Tupperware Fix and Mix. Bring following to a boil:

2 sticks butter
1 C. white sugar
1 C. brown sugar

1/2 C. white Karo
1 t. salt
1 t. vanilla

Boil for 5 minutes. Remove from heat and stir in 1 t. soda. Pour popcorn in roaster and stir in caramel sauce. Bake in warm oven, not over 250°, for 1 hour. Stir every 15 minutes.

Mrs. J.L. Miller

Crispy Caramel Corn

7 qt. popped corn
2 C. brown sugar
½ C. white Karo
1 t. salt

2 sticks oleo
½ t. soda
1 t. vanilla

Boil brown sugar, Karo, oleo and salt 5 minutes. Remove from stove and add soda and vanilla. Pour over popped corn in large mixing bowl and put in oven for 1 hour at 250°. Stir several times.

Mrs. Andy A. Yoder
Mrs. Atlee J. Miller

Mrs. Clara Mast
Mrs. Aden J. Hershberger
Mrs. Adam Yoder

Cheerio Squares

3 oz. pkg. jello (any flavor)
⅓ C. corn syrup
2 T. oleo
4 C. Cheerios

Butter 9 inch square pan. In a large saucepan blend jello, syrup and oleo. Heat to boiling over medium heat, stirring constantly. Remove from heat. Stir in Cheerios. Spread mixture in pan and let set about 30 minutes. Cut in squares.

Anna Kay Bowman
Mrs. Nelson A. Barkman

Marshmallow Creme Fudge

1 jar marshmallow creme
⅔ C. evaporated milk
1½ C. sugar

¼ C. butter or margarine
¼ t. salt

Combine all ingredients and bring to full boil, stirring constantly. Remove from heat. Add 2 C. chocolate chips and stir until melted. Stir in ½ C. chopped nuts and 1 t. vanilla. Pour into greased 8" square pan. Chill till firm. Makes 2¼ lbs.

Mrs. Levi Beachy

Rocky Road Bars

Put in double boiler: ½ C. butter, 1 C. powdered sugar, 1 egg, beaten, 1 pkg. chocolate or butterscotch chips. Stir until melted. Cool slightly and add 2-3 C. miniature marshmallows. Line bottom of pan with graham crackers and pour mixture on top.

Mrs. Nelson A. Barkman

Caramel Candy

2 C. white sugar
½ lb. oleo

1 C. white Karo
1 can Eagle Brand milk

Melt oleo, add sugar and Karo and bring to a boil. Take off heat and add milk. Bring to a soft ball stage. Pour in buttered 9" x 9" pan.

Rice Krispie Candy

¼ C. margarine or butter
4 C. miniature marshmallows
6 C. Rice Krispies

Melt butter and marshmallows together in double boiler. Stir in Rice Krispies. Press in buttered pan. Cut in desired sizes.

Mrs. Henry E. Schlabach

Peanut Butter Cups

2 C. peanut butter
2 lbs. powdered sugar

¼ C. butter
water (if necessary)

Put melted chocolate in little paper cups. While chocolate is still warm, put in a piece of peanut butter mixture which has been rolled in a thin log and sliced off. Then top with chocolate again. Makes over 200 small cups.

Mrs. Nelson A. Barkman

Peanut Butter Krispie Balls

2 C. peanut butter
2 sticks oleo
4 C. Rice Krispies

½ t. salt
4 C. powdered sugar

Melt oleo, stir in peanut butter and salt. Add Rice Krispies and enough powdered sugar to form a ball. Dip in chocolate.

Mrs. Nelson A. Barkman

Budget Fudge Candy

4½ C. white sugar
2 pkgs. potato chips (any flavor)
1 pt. marshmallow creme

1 can evaporated milk
1 lb. English walnuts
2 t. vanilla

Bring sugar and milk to a rolling boil. Cook 7 minutes, stirring constantly. Remove from heat and add remaining ingredients. Pour into buttered pan. Cool and cut in squares.

Mrs. Aden J. Hershberger

Yum Yum Candy

2 C. peanut butter
2 C. powdered sugar

3 C. Rice Krispies
¼ C. butter

Combine and mix all ingredients together and roll into balls. Dip in chocolate. Do not melt butter on stove.

Mrs. Adam Yoder

Fantasy Fudge

3 C. white sugar
3/4 C. Parkay margarine
2/3 C. evaporated milk
12 oz. pkg. chocolate chips or butterscotch chips
7 oz. jar marshmallow creme
1 C. chopped nuts
1 t. vanilla

Combine sugar, margarine and milk in heavy 2 1/2 qt. saucepan. Bring to full rolling boil, stirring constantly. Cook 5 minutes over medium heat. Remove from heat and stir in chocolate chips or butterscotch chips until melted. Add marshmallow creme, nuts and vanilla. Beat until well blended. Pour in a greased 13" x 9" pan. Cool. Cut in squares. Makes 3 lbs.

Mrs. Andy C. Yoder

Brown Sugar Divinity

1 C. brown sugar
1 C. white sugar
1/4 C. light Karo
1/2 C. water

pinch of salt
1/2 t. vanilla
1 1/2 C. nuts
2 egg whites

Combine first five ingredients in saucepan. Stir until sugar is dissolved, then cook without stirring till it forms a hard ball when put in cold water. Beat egg whites until stiff. Slowly beat in syrup. When it begins to thicken add vanilla. Beat until it holds its shape when dropped from a spoon. Add nuts and drop by teaspoon on buttered pan or wax paper.

Mrs. Andy C. Yoder

Krispie Bars

Melt 1 lb. chocolate, add 2 C. Rice Krispies. Spread into buttered jelly roll pan. Cut while warm. When cooled, remove and store in tight container.

Katie Coblentz

Magic Penuche Log

Penuche Filling

1¼ C. white sugar	¼ C. butter
¾ C. firmly packed brown sugar	1 t. vanilla
¼ t. salt	¾ C. chopped walnuts
⅔ C. milk	

Coating

4 C. puffed wheat	3 C. miniature
3 T. butter	marshmallows

For filling: Combine sugars, salt and milk in saucepan. Cook slowly until sugar is dissolved, stirring occasionally. Continue cooking without stirring to soft ball stage (236°). Remove from heat and add butter and vanilla. DO NOT STIR. Cool at room temperature to warm (110°) without stirring. Beat vigorously until mixture becomes thick and loses its gloss. Stir in walnuts. Shape to form a roll about 10 inches long. Roll in wax paper, refrigerate until firm (about 2 hours).

For coating: Heat puffed wheat in shallow pan at 350° for 10 minutes. Pour into greased bowl. Melt butter and marshmallows over low heat. Pour over puffed wheat, stirring until evenly coated. With greased hands shape mixture around penuche filling to form a log. Refrigerate 1 hour. Slice.

Mary Esta Yoder

Crunchy Treat

3 lbs. milk chocolate	2 C. peanut butter
2 lbs. butterscotch coating	1 box Rice Krispies or
	Rice Chex

Have peanut butter and rice cereal at room temperature. Melt chocolate and butterscotch. Stir in peanut butter. Cool till only slightly warm then mix in rice cereal and spread ¾ inch thick on wax paper. When firm cut in squares.

Mrs. Nelson A. Barkman

Rice Krispie Treats

1 C. sugar
1 C. white Karo
1 C. chocolate chips

1 C. peanut butter
6 C. Rice Krispies
1 C. butterscotch chips

Heat sugar and Karo and bring to a boil. Remove from heat. Add peanut butter and Rice Krispies. Press into greased pan. Melt chocolate chips and butterscotch chips and pour over Krispie mixture.

Ruth Ann Frey
Mrs. David D. Miller

- *Favorite Recipes* -

- Notes -

Miscellaneous

Pizza Sauce

Cook ½ bushel tomatoes. Chop 5 onions and add 4 hot peppers to tomatoes, cook to soup stage for 2½ hours. Then run through sieve. Add:

1 C. cooking oil	1½ C. white sugar
1 T. basil	½ t. salt
1 T. oregano	

Cook another hour. Then add 4 (12 oz.) cans tomato paste. Bring to boil. Pack in hot jars and seal.

Mrs. Fannie Yoder

Sauce for Hamburgers

Fry hamburger and mix the following sauce and pour over hamburger and simmer 45 minutes.

Sauce

1 C. catsup	2 T. vinegar
2 T. brown sugar	2 T. Worcestershire sauce

Mrs. John A. Miller

Sandwich Spread

6 large onions	6 red peppers
6 green tomatoes	6 green peppers

Grind, mix in 1 large T. salt. Let drain 1 hour. Put in 1 qt. vinegar and 1 qt. water and boil 15 minutes. Add 1 C. flour, 5 C. white sugar, 1 T. turmeric and 1 pt. mustard. Boil 5 minutes. Put in jars and seal.

Mattie Hershberger

Sandwich Spread

6 green tomatoes   1 onion
6 peppers (all colors)

Grind together and drain. Add ½ C. mustard, ½ C. vinegar, 1½ C. white sugar and ½ T. celery seed. Boil 10 minutes. Add ½ C. flour. Bring to boil. Remove from heat and stir in 1 pt. salad dressing and can it.

Mrs. Fannie Yoder

Pepper Relish

12 red peppers   12 onions
12 green peppers

Grind together fine with food grinder. Pour boiling water over it until covered. Let stand 15 minutes. Then drain and add:

1 qt. vinegar   2 T. salt
5 C. white sugar   2 oz. mustard seed

Cook for 20 minutes. Put in jars and seal.

Mrs. Andy C. Yoder

Cucumber Relish

6 lg. cucumbers   1 T. mustard seed
4 lg. onions   ½ t. turmeric
4 lg. peppers   2 C. vinegar
2 T. salt   5 C. sugar
1 T. celery seed   2 drops green coloring

Grind cucumbers, onions and peppers. Mix in salt and let set overnight. Drain and rinse. Add remaining ingredients. Cook slowly until thick and most of juice has boiled away, approximately 30-40 minutes. Pack in sterilized jars. Yields 3 pints.

Mary Esta Yoder

Bar-B-Q Sauce

1 pt. vinegar
1 pt. warm water
1 pt. Crisco oil

4 oz. salt
2 T. Worcestershire sauce

Boil together and spray on halves as you barbecue. Enough for 10-12 chicken halves.

Mrs. Fannie Yoder

B-B-Q Sauce for Chicken

1/2 C. vinegar
5 T. salt
1/2 lb. butter or oleo

2 T. Worcestershire sauce
1 C. wine

Boil together and spray on chicken as you barbecue.

Mrs. Daniel Barkman

Bar-B-Q Chicken Sauce

1/2 lb. butter or oleo (1 C.)
1 pt. water
1 pt. vinegar

4 T. salt
2 T. Worcestershire sauce
1/2 t. Tabasco sauce

Bring to a boil. Spray on chicken as you barbecue.

Mrs. Dannie H. Burkholder

Pizza Sauce

15 C. tomato juice
3 onions
3 t. oregano
2 t. black pepper

1 1/2 C. white sugar
1 C. Wesson oil
6-7 T. flour
2 (12 oz.) cans tomato paste

Mix all together and bring to a boil. Put in jars and cold pack for 30 minutes.

Mattie Hershberger

Heinz Catsup

1 peck tomatoes
3 large onions

Boil till soft then run through food mill. Drain in bag for 2 hours. Take the thick part and add:

4 C. white sugar
3 t. salt
1 pt. vinegar
Tie spice in cloth:
1/2 t. cloves
1/2 t. cinnamon
1/2 t. dry mustard

Boil 10 minutes. Bottle and seal.

Mrs. Henry M. Troyer

Catsup

1 gal. tomato juice
1 T. ground mustard
1 t. black pepper
1 T. allspice
1 T. salt
1 C. vinegar
3 C. sugar
1/4 t. garlic salt

Boil down to 1/2 amount or to desired thickness. Put in jars and seal while hot.

Mrs. John A. Weaver

Tomato Soya Sauce

1 peck tomatoes, sliced. Add 1/2 C. salt over these and 8 onions, sliced. Let set overnight. Drain juice the next morning and cook till tender. Put through colander. Add 1 pt. vinegar, 1 t. ginger, 1/2 t. black pepper, 1 t. cinnamon, 1 t. cloves and 1 t. mustard. Cook 2 hours slowly and add 2 lb. sugar. Process 10 minutes.

Mary Schlabach

233

Brine Recipe

Soak meat: chicken, turkey, a whole pig (around 40 lb. of any meat you prefer) in 1 C. Tenderquick, 1½ C. Morton sugar cure and 1½ gal. water. Keep in a cool place for 5-6 days. Drain and bake in oven until tender. If you don't have Morton sugar cure use 1 C. Tenderquick, ½ C. brown sugar and ¼ C. liquid smoke. The first recipe is the best. Try it.

Mrs. Melvin E. Mast

Pizza Sauce

3 onions, cut fine
1 C. white sugar
1 t. garlic salt
1 can mushroom soup

3 small cans tomato paste
3 lb. can tomato soup
3 qts. tomato juice

Mix all together and put in jars. Cold pack 30 minutes. Makes 12 pints.

Mrs. Henry E. Mast

Barbecue Sauce for Hamburger

1 C. catsup
1 T. vinegar

2 T. sugar
2 T. Worcestershire sauce

Mrs. Henry E. Mast

Pizza & Spaghetti Sauce

3 med. onions, cut fine
1 C. white sugar
1 t. garlic salt
2 T. oregano leaves
1-2 cans mushroom soup

3 (6 oz.) cans tomato paste
5 cans tomato soup
3 qts. tomato juice
2 green peppers

Dice green peppers and cook in tomato juice. Put everything in a big bowl and stir together. Put in jars and cold pack for 30 minutes. Makes 12 pints or 6 quarts.

Mrs. Marlin Yoder

Hot Chocolate Sauce

1 C. white sugar
1 C. water
3 T. cocoa

3 T. flour
1/8 t. salt

Cook 3 minutes and add vanilla. Very good over ice cream.

Mrs. Delbert R. Troyer

Butter Barbecue Sauce

1/2 C. butter
1/2 C. chopped onions
1/2 C. catsup
1/4 C. light brown sugar (packed)

3 T. Worcestershire sauce
1 1/2 t. chili powder
1/8 t. pepper
dash of Tabasco sauce

In a qt. saucepan melt butter. Add onions and saute until tender. Stir in remaining ingredients. Simmer 5 minutes. Sauce keeps well in refrigerator. Warm before using.

Mrs. Eli A. Beachy

Peach Jam

6 C. peaches, chopped
6 C. white sugar

2 C. crushed pineapple

Cook together 20 minutes. Add 6 oz. orange jello. Put in jars and seal or cold pack a few minutes.

Mrs. Henry D. Miller

Peach Jam

6 C. peaches, finely mashed or chopped
6 C. white sugar
2 C. crushed pineapple

Cook 20 minutes and add 6 oz. orange jello. Put in jars and seal or cold pack a few minutes.

Mrs. Eli D. Miller

Rhubarb Jam

5 C. rhubarb
5 C. sugar

Let set overnight. Cook 5 minutes and add 2 (3 oz.) boxes strawberry jello. Add 1 C. water.

Mrs. Nelson A. Barkman

Marshmallow Topping

2 C. white sugar   1 C. water
2½ C. light Karo
Cook to 253° then cool 5 minutes. Add:
⅞ C. egg whites (¾ C. plus 1 egg white = ⅞ C.)
½ C. light Karo

While the first part is cooking, mix and beat the second part—egg whites and Karo. Pour syrup over this and stir till cool. Vanilla may be added if you wish.

Mrs. Dannie H. Burkholder

Church Spread

2 C. white sugar   2 C. light Karo
2 C. brown sugar   2 C. dark Karo

Boil 2 minutes. When cool but not cold add 5 egg whites, beaten stiff, and stir until cold.

Mrs. Adam Yoder

Church Spread

4 lb. white sugar   1 qt. dark Karo
1 lb. brown sugar   3 qt. light Karo
pinch of cream of tartar

Mix all together and cook till boiling. Let stand till cool and add 8 beaten egg whites. Do not stir while cooking.

Mrs. Atlee J. Miller

Best Sugar Spread
For Church

2 C. brown sugar   2 C. light Karo
1 C. white sugar   1 C. dark Karo

Boil this just a little, pour slowly into 3 egg whites, stiffly beaten. Stir till cool.

Mrs. Eli A. Beachy

Peanut Butter for Church

10 C. brown sugar   ³/₄ C. light Karo
5 C. water

Boil 10-15 minutes. Cool. Add 3 qt. marshmallow creme and 5-6 lb. peanut butter.

Mrs. Mose M. Miller

Homemade Honey

5 lb. white sugar
1¹/₂ pt. water

Boil till clear (approx. 5 minutes). Add 1 t. alum. Remove from stove and add 85 red clover blossoms or 100 white blossoms. Let stand 10 minutes. Strain out blossoms. Tastes like honey.

Mrs. David D. Miller

Apple Butter

3 gal. apple slices, not cooked
8 lbs. white sugar
¹/₂ gal. dark Karo
1 gal. light Karo

Cook slowly 4 hours. Put lid on till it cooks. Put through sieve and add 1¹/₂ t. cinnamon. Put in jars and cold pack 10 minutes. Makes 3 gallons.

Mrs. David D. Miller

Corncob Syrup

6 red corncobs, washed. Break in pieces. Boil 1 hour in 3 qt. water. Strain and add 3 lb. brown sugar and water (enough to make 3 qt.). Boil until it starts to thicken or is consistency of maple syrup. Be sure to select clean corncobs free from mold. Light colored cobs make a lighter syrup and give a better flavor. Tastes just as good as maple syrup. Delicious!

Mrs. Atlee J. Miller

Crispy Pickles

1 gal. pickles, sliced. Add 1 gal. cold water with 1 C. salt. Let stand 3-5 days. Drain and wash in clear water. Add boiling water (enough to cover pickles) and 1 T. alum. Boil for 10 minutes. Drain and make syrup. Add syrup and boil for about 10 minutes. Put in jars and seal.

Syrup

1 pt. vinegar
1 pt. water
3 lbs. white sugar (6 C.)

Put in a spice bag:
1 T. celery seed
1 T. whole cloves
1 T. allspice
1 T. cinnamon

Katie N. Miller

Catsup

8 qt. tomato juice
7 C. white sugar
1/4 C. salt
2 C. ground onions
1 t. cinnamon
1 t. nutmeg
1 t. ginger
1/2 qt. vinegar (scant)

Boil until thick. Do not seal, just cork.

Mrs. Henry E. Mast

Bread and Butter Pickles

Slice thinly 1 gal. raw cucumbers and 4 small onions. Mix ½ C. salt with them and let stand 3 hours. Combine and add:

5 C. white sugar	1 t. celery seed
1½ t. turmeric	¾ C. vinegar
2 t. mustard seed	4 C. water

Heat and put in jars and seal. Makes 7 pt.

Mrs. David D. Miller

Sweet Dill Strips

Cover 2 dozen medium sized cucumbers with boiling water. Let set 4 hours. Cut strips lengthwise. Heat till boiling:

3 C. vinegar	4½ t. celery seed
¾ C. water	4½ t. turmeric
6 C. sugar	¾ t. mustard seed
3 T. salt	1 t. alum

Place fresh dill in bottom of jars. Pack solidly with cucumbers, top with another dill (I use dill seed). Add juice and seal. Yield: 6-8 quarts.

Edna Troyer

Refrigerator Pickles

7 C. unpeeled sliced cucumbers
1 C. diced green peppers
1 C. sliced onions
   Make a brine with:

1 C. vinegar	2 C. sugar
2 t. salt	1 T. celery seed

Mix vinegar and sugar. Do not heat. When sugar is dissolved, add celery seed and salt and pour over sliced cucumbers. Store in refrigerator in covered container. Let stand 24 hours before using.

Mrs. Merlin Troyer

Garlic Dill Pickles

Place 2 heads of dill in a quart jar. Fill jar with cucumbers. Place 2-3 garlic buds on top. Heat:

2 C. vinegar   3 C. sugar
3 t. salt

Bring to boil then pour over pickles. Cold pack just to boiling. Do not boil. Makes 3 quart. For crisp pickles, let cool in canner.

Mary Ellen Troyer

Lime Pickles

Slice 7 lbs. pickles. Put in 2 C. pickling lime and 2 gal. cold water. Let stand overnight then rinse 3 times. Put in cold water 3 hours, drain, then put in solution of 2 qt. vinegar (scant), 4½ lbs. white sugar, 2 T. salt, 2 t. pickling spice, 1 t. whole cloves, 1 t. mustard seed. Tie spice in a cloth. Simmer 30 minutes, put in hot jars and seal.

Mrs. Nelson A. Barkman

Cinnamon Stick Pickles

Peel, seed and slice pickles to make 2 gal. of sticks. Put in crock or enamel canner with 2 C. pickling lime and enough water to cover. Soak 24 hours. Drain and wash. Soak again in plain water for 4 hours. Drain and cover with the following: 1 C. vinegar, 1 T. alum, ½ bottle red food color and water to cover. Simmer for 2 hours. Drain and throw away liquid.

Syrup
1 T. salt, 2 C. water, 2 C. vinegar, 12oz. pkg. of red cinnamon candy, 10 C. white sugar. Bring to a boil and pour over cooked pickles. Let stand for 24 hours. Drain and bring syrup to a boil again. Pour over pickles. Do this 4 days. Drain and pack in jars. Heat syrup to a boil and pour in jars and cold pack 10 minutes.

Mrs. Nelson A. Barkman

Dill Pickles

1 qt. vinegar	2 T. mustard seed
4 qt. water	1½ T. pickling spice
1 C. salt	¾ C. sugar

Mix above ingredients. Then add to bottom of each jar:

1 sprig dill	1 clove garlic
3 slices onions	

Fill jars with small cucumbers. Pour vinegar mix over cucumbers and cold pack till water starts to boil. Remove jars from hot water immediately.

Mrs. David R. Yoder

Sliced Sweet Pickles

Soak 2 gallons sliced cucumbers in cold water with 2 C. salt for 4 days. Drain cold water and cover with boiling water. Let set till next day. Drain and cover with hot water in which has been added 1 rounded T. alum. Let set 1 day and drain and rinse well with cold water. Drain well then add hot syrup made of:

1½ qt. water
½ qt. vinegar
14 C. white sugar
2 T. mixed pickle spice
1 t. turmeric
1 t. celery seed

Pour this hot syrup off and reheat for 3 days in a row. Pack in jars, add juice and cold pack just to boiling.

Mrs. Eli M. Yoder

Sweet Dill Pickles

1 qt. vinegar	¼ C. salt
1 pt. water	4 onions, sliced or chopped
4 C. white sugar	

Cook this together a few minutes then fill 5 qt. jars with sliced pickles. Put 3 little garlic seeds in each jar then pour hot vinegar mix over pickles and cold pack 5 minutes. This is very good.

Lizzie Raber

241

Mixed Pickle

2 qt. small lima beans
2 qt. large lima beans
1 qt. carrots, sliced
1 qt. kidney beans
2 heads cauliflower
1 qt. celery, sliced
2 qt. pickles

1 qt. onions, chopped or
  sliced
1 qt. string beans
6 each red, yellow and
  green peppers, chopped
  or sliced

Cut up vegetables separately. Cook each in salt water till tender. Drain. Put in cold water and drain. Add cooked shell macaroni. Put spices in cheesecloth and cook in sugar vinegar mix.

Spices

2 t. celery seed
2 cinnamon sticks

1 T. pickle mix

Sugar Vinegar Mix

5 C. sugar or more
2 C. vinegar
4 C. water

1-2 T. turmeric
1 T. clear jel

Cold pack ½ hour.

Katie N. Miller

Red Beets

6 C. water from beets
6 C. vinegar
14 C. white sugar
7 t. salt

Cook beets in water then use beet water to make syrup to can. Slice or put whole beets in jars, add hot syrup and seal. Add mixed pickling spice as desired.

Mrs. J.L. Miller

- *Favorite Recipes* -

- Notes -

Drinks

Red Ribbon Punch

46 oz. can red Hawaiian Punch
6 oz. can frozen pineapple juice
28 oz. bottle chilled 7-Up
2 bottles Faygo orange pineapple pop
1 qt. pineapple sherbet

Double this recipe to make a punch bowl full. Freeze 2 rings punch in a ring to use while serving.

Mary Ellen Troyer

Hot Cocoa Mix

5 C. dry milk
6 oz. Cremora
1 C. powdered sugar
2 C. Nestle's Quik chocolate

Mix together and put in tight container. Keeps a long time. To use put 1/3 C. mix in a cup filled with hot water.

Mrs. Henry D. Miller
Mrs. Emanuel H. Yoder

Purple Cow

Combine in a shaker:

1 C. grape juice, chilled   3-5 T. milk
2-3 T. sugar (optional)
   Shake well and add:
2 large scoops vanilla ice cream

Shake until blended or put in blender. Pour into cold glasses and serve with a smile.

Mrs. Merlin Troyer

Orange Julius

6 oz. frozen orange juice	¼ C. sugar
1 C. milk	½ t. vanilla
1 C. water	10 ice cubes

Crush in blender until slushy.

Mrs. Merlin Troyer

Hot Chocolate Mix

11 oz. or 14 oz. jar Cremora
1 lb. box Nestle's Quik
1 box dry milk
1 C. powdered sugar

Mix well and store in covered container. Mixing ratio: 1 part mix and 2 parts hot water.

Mrs. Nelson A. Barkman

Instant Hot Chocolate

9 C. dry milk	6 oz. dry coffee creamer
1 lb. Nestle's Quik (3¼ C.)	2 C. powdered sugar

Mix well and store in jars. Use 3 T. for each cup. Mix with hot water. 3-4 small marshmallows may be added to each cup.

Mrs. Jonas N. Borntrager

Grape Juice

12 C. water	6 C. grapes
2 C. white sugar	

Cook about 5 minutes. Put through cloth in colander or in bag to drain. Cold pack 15 minutes.

Mrs. Dan J. Bowman

Grape Juice

15 C. grapes
9 C. boiling water

Boil 5 minutes. Drain. Add 5 C. water to pulp. Drain again. Add 3½ C. sugar. Heat to boiling and can.

Mary Ellen Troyer

Summer Grape Drink

2 qt. grapes. Cover with water and 2 T. vinegar. Let stand 1 hour then boil a little and strain. Take half as much sugar as juice and bring to a boil. Put in bottles. When ready to serve, add water.

Mrs. Levi Beachy

Quick Root Beer

2 C. white sugar
1 gal. lukewarm water

3 t. root beer extract
1 t. dry yeast

Use some hot water to dissolve sugar. Put in jars. Cover and set in sun for 4 hours. Chill before serving. Ready to serve next day.

Mrs. Aden J. Hershberger

Frozen Pops

1 pkg. jello
1 envelope Kool-Aid
1 C. sugar

2 C. boiling water
2 C. cold water

Dissolve jello, Kool-Aid and sugar in boiling water then add cold water and freeze.

Mrs. Adam Yoder

- *Favorite Recipes* -

- Notes -

Canning, Etc.

Sauerkraut

Shred cabbage like for slaw. Press tight in quart jars. Fill jars with boiling water. For 1 qt. add 2 t. vinegar, 1 t. salt and 1 t. white sugar. Cover and let set for 6 weeks. Cold pack for 30 minutes.

Mattie Hershberger

To Can Sauerkraut

Shred cabbage and put in jars (not tightly). Make a hole down through center and put 1 T. salt in. Pour boiling water over it and it will seal. Leave set for 6 weeks and it should be ready.

Mrs. Emma Hershberger

Canning Strawberries

7 qt. crushed strawberries
4 C. sugar
5 T. clear jel

1 C. strawberry jello
3 C. water

Mix strawberries and sugar. Set aside. Cook together jello, clear jel and water. Add to strawberries. Put in jars and cold pack 10 min. Let set in canning water until cool.

Mrs. John A. Weaver

Homemade Bologna

Use one big dishpan to mix 25 lb. fresh hamburger, ³/₄ lb. Tenderquick and 1 qt. warm water. Let stand overnight. Next morning add:

1 T. pepper
1 big handful seasoning salt
¹/₂ C. sugar
1 t. garlic
1 t. liquid smoke
1 qt. warm water

Mix all together, put in jars and cold pack 2 hours.

Mrs. Jonas A.M. Yoder

To Put Bologna in Salt Water

1 C. salt   1 gal. boiling water
1 T. brown sugar

Cool and put in bologna. This keeps for up to 1½-2 months or more.

Mrs. David D. Miller

Canning Meat Chunks with Tenderquick

1 gal. water   4-5 gal. meat chunks
1 lb. Tenderquick

Soak the above for 2-3 days. Put in jars then fill with clear water and add no salt. Cold pack 3 hours.

Mrs. Nelson A. Barkman

Recipe to Soak Steak for Barbecue

1 C. soy sauce   3-6 whole cloves
1 t. ginger   3 garlic bulbs or scant
1 t. dry mustard   ½ t. garlic powder
½ C. salad oil   1 t. Accent

Mix and pour over steak.

Mrs. John A. Miller

Canning Apples for Pie

12 C. apples, sliced, or put through Salad Master
5 C. white sugar
6 T. minute tapioca
3 C. water

Mix together and cold pack 15 minutes. Don't make jars quite full. Grimes or Golden Delicious are best.

Mrs. Nelson A. Barkman

To Can Sweet Corn

Cut off corn, put in dish and add salt and some white sugar. Stir till well mixed. Press in jars and put a fresh slice tomato on top. Cold pack 3 hours. Don't add any water to sweet corn, and don't heat before canning.

Mrs. Nelson A. Barkman

Fruit Cocktail to Can

1 bushel peaches
1 bushel pears
2 gal. tidbit pineapple
10 lbs. white grapes, cut in half
maraschino cherries, cut in half

Mix all together. Add sugar syrup that was made to suit your taste. Mix well and put in jars and cold pack 15 minutes. Makes 50 quarts.

Mrs. Albert M.L. Yoder

Catsup Spice

2 T. cinnamon
1 T. cloves
2 t. allspice

½ t. cayenne pepper
3 T. paprika
1 t. nutmeg

4 T. = 1oz. spice

Mix all together.

Mrs. Nelson A. Barkman

To Can Strawberries

3 qt. mashed berries (not fine)
1½ C. sugar
1 box Danish Dessert

Mix together, put in jars, cold pack 10 minutes. Let stand in water till water is cold, then take out.

Mrs. Dan J. Bowman

Strawberry Preserves

4 C. crushed strawberries
7 C. sugar

Cook 10 minutes then add 1 t. Epsom salt. Skim, put in jars and seal. Yield: 4 pt.

Mary Esta Yoder

Pineapple Preserves

1 qt. crushed pineapple
1 qt. light Karo

5 lb. white sugar

Cook 5 minutes. Put in jars while hot and seal.

Mrs. Nelson A. Barkman

Canned Suckers

Scale fish (don't skin). Split in half down the back. Cut into about 2" pieces. Wash well and let drain overnight. Keep cool. Pack pieces into sterilized 1 qt. jars (prefer wide mouth) Add 1 1/4 t. salt, 1/4 C. vinegar and 4 T. catsup. Pack fish firmly into jars so the ingredients cover fish. Take butter knife and poke all the ingredients you can along the inside of the jar then seal jar. Put in cold pack canner and boil slowly for 6 hours which will soften the bones. You can use a wash boiler but put something under jars to raise off bottom about 1/2". Will turn red and taste like salmon.

Mrs. Henry E. Mast

- *Notes* -

Home Remedies & Preparing Wild Game

Knox Gelatine
For Flower Plants

Dissolve 1 pkg. Knox gelatine in 1 C. hot water. Add 3 C. cold water. Makes 1 quart. Use to water flower plants once a month.

Mrs. Nelson A. Barkman

Play Dough

2 C. flour
$\frac{1}{2}$ C. cornstarch
1 T. powdered alum

2 C. water
1 C. salt
1 T. salad oil

Place all ingredients in saucepan. Stir constantly over low heat until mixture thickens into dough consistency. Remove from heat and let cool until it can be handled. Place on Formica top and knead like bread until smooth. Add food coloring if you wish. Store in tight container or plastic bag. This recipe keeps for months, is safe and nontoxic.

Mary Schlabach

Whooping Cough Medicine

1 lemon, sliced thin
1 qt. water
$\frac{1}{2}$ pt. flax seeds

Simmer 3-4 hours. Do not boil. Strain while hot. Add 2 oz. honey then water to make 1 pt. Dosage: 1 T. 4 times a day. In addition a dose after each severe fit of coughing.

Mrs. Nelson A. Barkman

Cough Syrup

Put 3 whole eggs in the shell in a pint jar and fill with vinegar. Put a jar flat on top but do not screw lid on. Let stand 4-5 days till the shell gets soft and slightly black. Lift eggs out and fill the jar up with honey. Mix and use. Dosage: 1 t. 4 times a day.

Mrs. Nelson A. Barkman

Pantry Plant Food
For Flower Plants

1 t. baking powder
1 t. Epsom salt

1 t. saltpeter
$^1/_2$ t. household ammonia

Stir together and mix with 1 gallon of lukewarm water. Water with this in place of regular watering every 4-6 weeks. This works very well to perk up houseplants, especially vines and ivys.

Mrs. Nelson A. Barkman

Snake Bites

Beat the yolk of a fresh egg and mix with salt to the consistency of a good salve. Apply to the bite as a poultice and change frequently till poison is all out.

Boil water and fill small bottle $^1/_4$ full and hold against fang marks to draw out poison.

Take enough vinegar and salt to dip up with the hand. Lay the salt on the bite and keep it on till the poison is drawn out. Don't give the patient anything in stomach till poison is drawn out. This is good for man and beast.

For snake bites, stings or any poisonous bites. Pound a lot of onions till soft, salt liberally and bind on as a poultice. Change often.

Bee Stings

Cover infected parts with dampened salt.

Soak with Listerine.

Make thick paste of baking soda and water and let dry.

If away from the house put wet clay or mud on sting.

Vicks applied to sting will give relief.

Fainting

A drink of vinegar is a sure cure for fainting.

Earache

Dip cotton in molasses, put in ear and the pain will cease.

Sore Throat

Take vinegar and make it strong with salt and red pepper (black may be used) and gargle often.

Arthritis

10 t. apple cider vinegar to a glass of water at each meal. Use honey instead of sugar.

High Blood Pressure

Eat apples, grapes, cranberries or their juice. Eat a small amount of honey at each meal.

Spring Tonic

Mix sulfur, cream of tartar and Epsom salts in a jar of water. Take 2-3 swallows each morning.

Bites and Stings

Mad Dog: Wash the bitten part in vinegar and water 2-3 times a day. Give a teaspoonful of vinegar and water every morning for 2-3 days.

Lemonade Diet
(Cleanse your system)

2 T. lemon juice $1/_{10}$ t. red pepper
2 T. maple syrup

We take red pepper in capsules. Combine the juice and maple syrup in a 10 oz. glass and fill with hot water (cold water may be used if desired). Drink 6-12 glasses a day. 2 t. sea salt to a quart of lukewarm water. First day after diet: Several 8 oz. glasses of fresh orange juice as desired during the day. Drink it slowly. Second Day: Drink several glasses of orange juice during the day, with extra water if needed. In the afternoon prepare vegetable soup by boiling together potatoes, carrots and celery. Have this soup for the evening meal, using the broth mostly. Third Day: Drink orange juice in the morning and at noon. Have some more soup in the evening. Eat whatever is desired in the form of vegetables, salads or fruit. No meat or eggs, bread or pastries.

Fried Frog Legs

Only the hind legs of frogs can be eaten. Cut off the feet, peel off skin, turning inside out. Wipe with cold damp cloth, season with salt and pepper. Roll in flour. Dip in well beaten eggs diluted with little water. Roll in cracker crumbs. They may be dipped in fritter batter instead, in which case omit flour and eggs. Fry in deep hot fat until golden brown, about 3 minutes. Serve with tartar sauce. If desired, legs may be seasoned by soaking in a mixture of lemon juice, salt and pepper 1 hour before rolling in flour.

Mast Printing

Roasted Rabbit

Use young rabbits weighing 2-3 lbs. They should be skinned and cleaned as soon as possible after killing. Wash thoroughly and dry. Stuff with poultry stuffing. Dampen. Sew opening. Tie or fasten legs close to the body. Place on side in roaster. Roast in hot oven (450°) for 15 minutes. Turn once and baste frequently with melted butter or drippings. Reduce heat and continue cooking in moderate oven (350°) for 1$1/4$-1$1/2$ hours. Baste every 15 minutes.

Mast Printing

Roasted Goose

8-10 lb. goose
1$1/2$ t. salt
$1/4$ t. pepper
2 C. celery stuffing
6 thin strips fat salt pork

Dress goose, wash thoroughly and dry. Stuff and sprinkle with salt and pepper. Tie and sew securely with wings and legs close to body. Put breast up, in roasting pan with strips of pork on top. Bake in quick oven (450°) for 15 minutes. Add 1 C. water and baste. Reduce heat to 350° and cook 20 minutes per pound, basting every 15 minutes. Remove pork strips during last 30 minutes of cooking. If desired goose may be rubbed with cut side of an onion or clove of garlic before cooking. Serve with gravy.

Mast Printing

Roasted Grouse

Pick, singe, dress and clean grouse, inside and out. Sprinkle with salt and pepper, brush with oil or fat. Tie wings and legs close to body. Put in roasting pan. Add 1 C. boiling water. If desired lay strip of bacon over bird. Bake in hot oven (450°) for 15 minutes, basting frequently with melted butter or pan drippings. Reduce heat and bake 25 minutes or more in moderate oven at 350°. Remove bird. Add a little flour mixed to a smooth paste with cold water, cook until well blended. While grouse is cooking, boil the livers, pound into a thick paste with butter, pepper, salt and some juice from pan. Spread this mixture on toast and serve grouse on top.

Mast Printing

'Tis Canning Time

'Tis canning time far and wide
Across this whole vast countryside.
They're carrying empties from below
Or toting full jars down to stow.
Mom has a feeling it's all right
To bottle everything in sight.
Our meals are lean and hurried up
While Mom fills up her measuring cup
With beans or peas or carrots gold
She knows next winter will be cold.
For these past months about everywhere
There's not a single inch to spare—
There's jars of beets and jars of corn
A-gathering there since early morn—
There's relish, pickles, catsup and jam
In fact as much as Mom could ram
In jars of every shape and size
That she could really utilize.
Mom says it isn't right to waste
What God provides, so she makes haste
From summertime till late in fall
The vegetables are in our own lot,
And everything the neighbors got
Our porch and kitchen overflow
And keep us running to and fro
With baskets full of everything
That has been grown since early spring.

(cont.)

There's running to the country store
For rubber rings and lids and more—
For spices, sugar, salt and wax
And won't let me and Dad relax—
There's pickles fat and pickles lean
And every kind of long string bean—
There's peas and white and yellow corn
That Dad and I have meekly borne
From garden patch and berry row.
And everywhere that we did hoe . . .
Oh, well, our cellar's nearly full
And I mean really bountiful,
And Mom's as happy as can be
That she went on this canning spree.
And I must own I really love
The smell of cinnamon and clove . . .
Of vinegar and spicy pears
And all the juices Mom prepares . . .
There's charm to canning time each year
With canning's special atmosphere...
But we know Mom; we know her mind
For she is merciful and kind . . .
Our shelves are loaded down today
But Mom will give about half away!

Table Rules

In silence I must take my seat
And give God thanks before I eat;
Must for my food in patience wait
Till I am asked to hand my plate.

I must not scold nor whine nor pout
Nor move my chair or plate about;
With knife or fork or napkin ring
I must not play, nor must I sing.

I must not speak a useless word
For children should be seen, not heard;
I must not talk about my food
Nor fret if I don't think it's good.

I must not say, "The bread is old,"
"The tea is hot," "The coffee cold,"
I must not cry for this or that
Nor murmur if my meat is fat.

My mouth with food I must not crowd
Nor while I'm eating speak aloud;
Must turn my head to cough or sneeze
And when I ask, say, "If you please."

The tablecloth I must not spoil
Nor with my food my fingers soil;
Must keep my seat till I am done
Nor round the table sport and run.

When told to rise, then I must put
My chair away with noiseless foot,
And lift my heart to God above
In praise for all His wondrous love.

God Has Blessed America

Our country God has richly blessed
With foods and eats so many,
So that it might be referred to as:
"The land of milk and honey."

But did we ever stop to think,
Not all lands have such wealth?
Some may be quite hungry
Not food enough for health.

While for our meals, we serve so much,
Rich foods we like to taste,
Then for our health it is not good
And perhaps some goes to waste.

Might we not displease our Lord,
Serving more than for our good?
Or would we show our thankfulness
By decorating food?

God has given; God could take!
It's all within His power.
We know not at all what might befall
Within a coming hour.

Some day, we might be made
To think back to our past,
If all the foods we wasted
We then could only grasp!

Yes, God has blessed America,
So let us try with prayer,
To use the blessings rightfully,
And with the needy share.

Index

Cakes *cont.*

Cookies

Cookies *cont.*

Salads *cont.*

Salads *cont.*

Main Dishes

Main Dishes *cont.*

Main Dishes *cont.*

Soups

Cereal, Etc.

Candy

Miscellaneous

Miscellaneous *cont.*

Drinks

Canning, Etc.

Canning, Etc. *cont.*

Home Remedies & Preparing Wild Game

Home Remedies & Preparing Wild Game *cont.*

Cooking with the Horse & Buggy People

Sharing a Second Serving of Favorites
from 207 Amish Women of Holmes County, Ohio

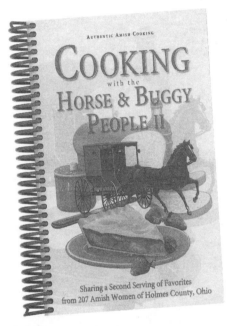

Henry and Amanda Mast, authors and compilers of *Cooking with the Horse and Buggy People Volume II* (as well as Volume I), live close to Charm, Ohio. Their home place is in the heart of the world's largest Amish community. The Masts and their friends worked countless hours in the kitchen to perfect the 600 recipes they chose to share with you.

Good food. Laughter. Compliments. Memories. That's what this new volume of *Cooking with the Horse and Buggy People* is about.

$11.99

· 5¹/₂" x 8¹/₂" · 320 pp · Spiral Bound · Extra-Heavy Laminated Cover
· ISBN 1-890050-62-8

Mary Yoder's Candy & Confections Cookbook

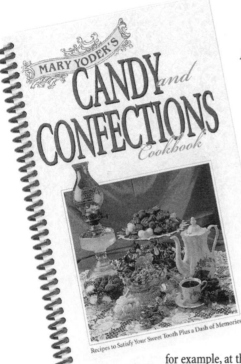

Mary Yoder

Ready for a really special treat …one that will satisfy your sweet tooth? Dripping chocolates, dreamy fudges, reach-for-more mints, and over 100 other sweet secrets—the homemade way. Mary has over 30 years' experience in making candy and confections—for her family as well as commercially. In this book she shares her own secret recipes, never before published.

Mary Yoder's Candy and Confections Cookbook is even more! Take a good look, for example, at the 24 color photos of the author's childhood memories and unique hobbies. You'll enjoy a walk down memory lane with her through the photos of her home, gardens, and hobbies. Seventy illustrations in her own original pencil art are scattered throughout the book.

The next time you need a treat so special, so unique, so mouthwatering that it can't be bought, reach for *Mary Yoder's Candy and Confections Cookbook*. You'll add that personal touch that's just right. You'll make that special moment even sweeter!

$9.99

· 5¹/₂" x 8¹/₂" · 126 pp · Spiral Bound · 24 Photographs
· 70 Original Pencil Illustrations by Mary Yoder · ISBN 1-890050-36-9

AUTHENTIC AMISH COOKING

The Wooden Spoon Cookbook

Meet 17-year-old Miriam Miller in the *Wooden Spoon Cookbook*. In addition to sharing her own, her mother's, and her grandmother's favorite recipes, Miriam shares childhood memories, stories, and personal details of her life as a young Amish girl.

$10.99

· 5¹/₂" x 8¹/₂" · 194 pp · Spiral bound · Laminated cover · Double indexed
· ISBN 1-890050-41-5

Amish Quilting
Cookbook

Sara Yoder

Fix up your favorite meal and enjoy the beauty of quilts at the same time with the new Quilting Cookbook. Its 130 pages are packed with 316 favorite recipes from 58 of Lone Star Quilt Shop's quilters. Twenty of their finest quilts are featured in color throughout the book. And the book is wrapped in a concealed spiral binding to help avoid spiral tangles while it keeps all the conveniences of traditional spiral.

$14.99
· 5¹/₂" x 8¹/₂" · 136 pp · Concealed Spiral
· ISBN 1-890050-73-3

Walnut Creek Valley

Less old-fashioned, more contemporary describes this one. Food preparation as it is today. These 700 authentic recipes are gleaned from the finest kitchens in Holmes County. We'll help you prepare food for large groups as well as your own dinner table. A special listing of quantities used in serving 100 people is on age 112. The canning and freezing section covers the subjects well! There are 11 sections in all.

$11.99

· 5½" x 8½" · 266 pp · Spiral bound · Indexed
· ISBN 1-890050-73-3

Give Us This Day Our Daily Bread

All the favorites of the Belle Center Amish Community. Over 600 of today's family favorites and even some from Grandma's kitchen. All the usual sections are here. But what makes this one special is the appetizers, large quantity recipes (for weddings, reunions, and other special occasions) and the children's recipe section. The tips, hints, and quotes section is filled with everyday kitchen secrets.

$11.99

· 5¹/₂" x 8¹/₂" · 263 pp · Spiral bound · Indexed
· ISBN 1-890050-73-3

Carlisle Press
WALNUT CREEK

2673 TR 421
Sugarcreek, OH 44681

TO ORDER COOKBOOKS

Check your local bookstore or call **1-800-852-4482.**